T0305554

Base of the Pyramid Markets in Asia

The Innovation and Sustainability in Base of the Pyramid Markets series comprises four volumes, covering theoretical perspectives, themes, and various aspects of interest across four key geographical regions where Base of the Pyramid (BOP) markets are located – Latin America, Asia, Africa, and affluent countries. This book focuses on the BOP markets in Asia, and in particular the challenge of how to address the needs of deprived population groups in a sustainable manner.

Base of the Pyramid Markets in Asia deals with, amongst other topics, the innovation and innovativeness that is necessary to better the life of resource-poor population groups. The book covers various themes and aspects of BOP markets in Asia and their embeddedness in socio-cultural settings, and adopts a variety of theoretical angles for analysing the phenomena. Thus, this book aims at furthering our understanding of BOP markets in Asia and at deriving valuable recommendations for managers and policy makers. BOP markets face unique challenges and private sector actors alone cannot ensure sustainable value creation activities. Multidimensional elements and factors are needed to alleviate poverty and create economic development aligned with principles of sustainable development. Therefore, the book comprises critical and empirical studies as well as conceptual papers on the challenges linked to BOP markets in Asian countries.

This book is recommended reading for managers and policy makers, as well as students and academics interested in Base of the Pyramid markets.

Marlen Gabriele Arnold is a Professor in the field of sustainability. Currently she holds the Chair for Corporate Environmental Management and Sustainability at the Chemnitz University of Technology, Germany.

Stefan Gold is Professor and Chair of Sustainability Management at the University of Kassel, Germany.

Judy N. Muthuri is an Associate Professor of Corporate Social Responsibility at Nottingham University Business School (NUBS), UK, and chairs the Social and Environmental Responsibility Group leading the School's UN Principles for Responsible Management Education work.

Ximena Rueda is an Associate Professor at the School of Management at the Universidad de los Andes, Colombia.

Innovation and Sustainability in Base of the Pyramid Markets

Series Editors:
Marlen Gabriele Arnold, Chemnitz University of Technology, Germany
Stefan Gold, Kassel University, Germany
Judy N. Muthuri, University of Nottingham, UK
Ximena Rueda, Universidad de los Andes, Colombia

Base of the Pyramid Markets in Asia
Innovation and Challenges to Sustainability
Edited by Marlen Gabriele Arnold, Stefan Gold, Judy N. Muthuri, and Ximena Rueda

For more information about this series, please visit https://www.routledge.com/Frugal-Innovation-in-Base-of-the-Pyramid-Markets/book-series/FINNBOP

Base of the Pyramid Markets in Asia

Innovation and Challenges to Sustainability

Edited by
Marlen Gabriele Arnold,
Stefan Gold,
Judy N. Muthuri, and
Ximena Rueda

Routledge
Taylor & Francis Group

LONDON AND NEW YORK

First published 2020 by Routledge

2 Park Square, Milton Park, Abingdon, Oxon OX14 4RN
605 Third Avenue, New York, NY 10017

Routledge is an imprint of the Taylor & Francis Group, an informa business

First issued in paperback 2021

British Library Cataloguing-in-Publication Data
A catalogue record for this book is available from the British Library

Library of Congress Cataloging-in-Publication Data
A catalog record has been requested for this book

ISBN: 978-1-138-38913-7 (hbk)
ISBN: 978-1-03-217451-8 (pbk)
DOI: 10.4324/9780429424151

Typeset in Bembo
by codeMantra

Contents

PART IV
Design, integration, innovation, and change of
BOP markets   93

Contributors

Sajid Amit, Director, Center for Enterprise and Society (CES), University of Liberal Arts Bangladesh (ULAB), Dhaka, Bangladesh. E-mail: sajid. amit@ulab.edu.bd

Marlen Gabriele Arnold, Professor of Corporate Environmental Management and Sustainability, Chemnitz University of Technology, Chemnitz, Germany. E-mail: marlen.arnold@wirtschaft.tu-chemnitz.de https://www. tu-chemnitz.de/wirtschaft/bwl8/

Usama Awan, Junior Researcher for Industrial Engineering and Management, Lappeenranta-Lahti University of Technology LUT, Lappeenranta, Finland. E-mail: usama.awan@lut.fi

Lumbini Barua, Research Associate, Center for Enterprise and Society (CES), University of Liberal Arts Bangladesh (ULAB), Dhaka, Bangladesh. E-mail: lumbini.barua@ulab.edu.bd

Tuba Bozaykut-Bük, Assistant Professor of Management, Istanbul Medipol University, Istanbul, Turkey. E-mail: tbozaykut@medipol.edu.tr

Janne Huiskonen, Professor of Industrial Engineering and Management (IEM), Lappeenranta-Lahti University of Technology LUT, Lappeenranta, Finland. E-mail: Janne.Huiskonen@lut.fi

Mina Mohammadi Khorasani, Freelance Journalist, Tehran, Iran. E-mail: meana.khorasani@gmail.com

Anne H. Koch, Professor of Global Strategy and Innovation, Hult International Business School, San Francisco, USA. E-mail: anne.koch@faculty. hult.edu

Andrzej Kraslawski, Professor of Industrial Engineering and Management (IEM), Lappeenranta-Lahti University of Technology LUT, Lappeenranta, Finland. E-mail: Andrzej.Kraslawski@lut.fi

Surendra Sah, Student at Chemnitz University of Technology, Chemnitz, Germany. E-mail: surendra.sah@wirtschaft.tu-chemnitz.de

Nazia Suleman, Assistant Professor, COMSATS University Islamabad, Islamabad, Pakistan. E-mail: NaziaSuleman@ciitvehari.edu.pk

Preface

Business concepts at the Base of the Pyramid (BOP) aim at creating value with and for the poor and, hence, represent one promising way of uplifting and integrating marginalised people. Private actors such as multinationals, small- and medium-sized enterprises, and entrepreneurs have a critical role to play in achieving the Sustainable Development Goals agenda as laid down by the United Nations in September 2015. Yet, BOP markets face unique challenges and private sector actors alone cannot ensure sustainable value creation activities. Multidimensional collaboration between various stakeholders, deep consumer behaviour insights, community-driven product, process and value chain design, knowledge and capabilities transfer, unanticipated outcomes of well-intended strategies of single actors etc. – all of these (and more …) are elements of the puzzle which still needs to be disentangled in order to alleviate poverty and create economic development aligned with principles of sustainable development. This motivated the development of a book series highlighting different regions. The BOP markets book series emerged as a result of global research and practical efforts covering theoretical perspectives, themes, and various aspects of interest of four main geographical regions where BOP markets are located – Asia, Africa, South America and the Caribbean, and affluent countries. The book series contributes to a profound understanding of BOP markets across the most important geographical areas around the world and presents insights on how the private sector can work together with other stakeholders to develop and operationalise economically viable business models in BOP markets while contributing to sustainable development. Therefore, the books comprise, among others, analytical and empirical studies, conceptual papers, and critical reflections on the challenges that are linked to BOP markets in the respective regions. Thereby, the book aims to cover the wide variety of different business environments, institutional and socio-cultural settings across the various countries and regions. A variety of stylistic elements, like research work, case studies, interviews or roundtable discussion, will give a wide and vivid impression of ongoing challenges and fruitful solutions.

As there are several theoretical approaches emphasising BOP contexts, we chose to follow network concepts. Network approaches aim at better understanding of new shapes of mixed partnership models, e.g. the partners' strategies, actions, and behaviour, and focus on the context, like drivers, enablers, missions or visions, main barriers and lifecycle stages, the configuration of BOP, like cooperation, structure, roles, relations, and patterns, and the capability of BOP, analysing the differences of key success factors and the design of networks, including integration, innovation, and change. Thus, the book series is organized in four main sections detailed below.

BOP markets

BOP markets are characterised by specific characteristics, there are core innovations, inclusive business models, main stakeholders and actors involved. As BOP markets are somehow related to frugal, reverse, and inclusive innovations that can foster a (sustainable) development and provide new business models and value streams that other countries can also benefit from, sustainable performance is not always clear and needs to be critically reflected.

Drivers and barriers of BOP markets

Institutional voids and mechanisms strongly influence BOP markets, both positively and negatively. Moreover, government and international intervention play a pivotal role in progressing BOP markets. Often business models fill in institutional gaps as strategies to scaling social and economic impact, trade-offs, and unanticipated outcomes.

Roles, cooperation, and structure in BOP markets

The configuration of BOP markets is closely linked to cooperation, structure, roles, relations, and patterns. Inclusive approaches, for instance, aim at participation, involvement, or cooperation between different market actors along the whole value chain. So, the analysis of (frugal) innovation networks, consumer behaviour, value co-creation, and cross-sector collaboration, the role of multinationals, innovation and knowledge capabilities, value co-creation and cross-sector collaboration, and women empowerment is pivotal for an understanding of BOP markets.

Design, integration, innovation, and change of BOP markets

The capabilities of BOP markets aim at the differences of key success factors of networks, the interactions concerning the management of design, production, procurement, and logistics, sustainable supply chains, and integration. The transformation of BOP markets is often accompanied by renewal, innovation, learning, intellectual property and global standards, social business, inclusive corporate social responsibility, circular business models, as well as approaches integrating sustainability.

The Asia edition is the first in a series of four books highlighting BOP markets around the globe, and is followed by Africa, South America and the Caribbean, and affluent countries. Asia has seen tremendous economic growth and increased social well-being in many parts; still there remains a substantial part of the population who suffer from poverty, insufficient education and health services, etc. This book focusses on the BOP in Asia, and in particular the challenge of how to address the needs of deprived population groups in a sustainable manner. It deals with, amongst others, innovation and innovativeness that is necessary to better the life of resource-poor population groups. The book covers various themes and aspects of BOP markets in Asia and their embeddedness in socio-cultural settings, and adopts a variety of theoretical angles for analysing the phenomena. Thus, this book aims at furthering our understanding of BOP markets in Asia and at deriving valuable recommendations for managers and policy makers. One important question hereby is how the private sector can work together with other stakeholders to develop and operationalise economically viable business models in BOP markets while contributing to sustainable development. This edition contains the following contributions.

In Chapter 1, Arnold and Sah provide insights into Asian BOP contexts by presenting interviews with BOP experts. In Chapter 2, Awan, Suleman, Huiskonen, and Kraslawski discuss the benefits of cross-border collaboration in BOP markets for innovation improvement. They argue for collaborative strategies to empower BOP markets in emerging economies and for improvements in innovation development. Anne Koch, in Chapter 3, highlights institutional voids and strategic responses by multinational corporations in BOP markets in Asia and critically reflects on how institutional voids act as barriers. She analyses how institutional voids can be influenced and used with strategic responses and opportunities for growth in Asian markets. In Chapter 4, Tuba Bozaykut-Bük covers business-NGO collaborations in Turkey. In her research, she examines business-NGO collaborations having the potential to influence social, economic, and working conditions of people at the BOP in Turkey. In Chapter 5, Amit and Barua discuss systemic constraints to financial inclusion in Bangladesh and Recommended Solutions. Their chapter focuses on the systemic constraints in the banking sector of Bangladesh, which impede financial inclusion of BOP people, by highlighting the case of ready-made garments (RMG) workers in Bangladesh. In Chapter 6, Mina Mohammadi Khorasani writes about the contribution and efficiency of social businesses in poverty reduction in Iran. She deals with the main causes of poverty in Iran, namely, inequality risen from dominant political-economy system, structural problems of public non-governmental organizations, inflation risen from governmental mismanagement, lack of investment in productive industrial sector, and unemployment.

Marlen Gabriele Arnold,
Chemnitz University of Technology, Germany

Stefan Gold,
University of Kassel, Germany

Judy N. Muthuri,
Nottingham University Business School, UK

Ximena Rueda,
Universidad de los Andes, Colombia
August 2019

Acknowledgements

As a peer-reviewed publication, the book has enormously benefited from the feedback and the comments from the reviewers. The editors express their gratitude to all reviewers involved, and thank them for their efforts, time, and constructive mindset. We also thank all authors and contributors of this volume for their valuable contributions, time, and effort. Finally, we are most grateful that Simon Fronczek supported organizational issues and formatting.

Part I

BOP markets

1 Insights into Asian Base of the Pyramid contexts

Interviews with BOP experts

Marlen Gabriele Arnold and Surendra Sah

Introduction

Countries mainly having higher levels of technology, education, expectation of life, basic services, food, etc. differ from countries that developed otherwise in a way generally having higher levels of poverty, specific diseases, less education, and limited basic services and expectation of life (Arnold, 2018). They differ in terms of innovation, business models, technology, and sustainability, as well as cooperation in science (Rosca, Arnold, & Bendul, 2016; Webb, Kistruck, Ireland, & Ketchen, 2010). Defining the Base of the Pyramid (BOP), Webb et al. (2010) identified differences in market characteristics within the BOP and stressed that BOP markets depend less on country boundaries than on formal or informal market characteristics. Like poverty, characteristics are: (a) low levels of education, skills, and capabilities, (b) weakly established infrastructure in urban areas, almost none in rural areas, (c) dominance of informal contracts and enforcement, including (d) minor property rights protection. Huge differences in design processes can be found between BOP and engineered markets (Jagtap et al., 2014; Silvestre & Silva Neto, 2014). Goods and services or even innovations offered in BOP markets often do not cause technological breakthroughs driving innovation in engineered markets (Zeschky, Winterhalter, & Gassmann, 2014; Brem & Wolfram, 2014; Soni & Krishnan, 2014). According to Govindarajan and Ramamurti (2011), BOP solutions focus on unique combinations of existing knowledge and technologies on local scales. In BOP research, the BOP 1.0 strategies, selling to the poor, or implying that multinational companies (MNCs) can reduce poverty by offering goods and services in BOP markets (Prahalad and Hammond 2002), changed to selling with the poor (BOP 2.0). In this perspective BOP or low-income consumers are involved in value creation processes (Simanis & Hart, 2008). The employment of locals enhances the chance to meet the customers' needs more precisely. Originally, the BOP 1.0 approach aimed at being an effective way to combat poverty and social exclusion through providing basic and functional goods and services at low costs in order to increase the standard of living. Yet, it did not appropriately mitigate poverty and social exclusion (Papaioannou, 2014). In addition, it was strongly criticised by non-governmental organizations (NGOs) and scientists (Shivarajan & Srinivasan,

2013). Currently, multinational corporations (MNCs), NGOs, and small and medium-sized enterprises (SMEs) are central players in BOP contexts (Arnold, 2018). BOP markets are characterised by various market participants. In the literature, BOP markets, including value creation and frugal innovation, are narrowly connected. Inclusive approaches aim at participation, involvement, or cooperation between different market actors along the whole value chain. Frugal innovation is a flexible design and production concept based on reduced costs and complexity. Many studies show that the BOP context is widely spread and diverse in Asia. The following interviews, conducted in the late autumn and winter of 2018, will give an insight into pivotal topics and current developments around BOP in Asia. In total, four experts were interviewed. Their knowledge and understanding of, as well as experience with, BOP contexts in Asia, are presented in the following.

The experts

Professor Jaideep Prabhu

Jaideep Prabhu (born October 12, 1967 in Bangalore, Karnataka, India) is the Jawaharlal Nehru Professor of Business and Enterprise at the Judge Business School at the University of Cambridge, England. Prof. Prabhu is also the Director of the Centre for India & Global Business (CIGB) whose Executive Director was Navi Radjou. He is the co-author of *Jugaad Innovation: Think Frugal, Be Flexible, Generate Breakthrough Growth*, described by The Economist as 'the most comprehensive book' on the subject of frugal innovation. Jaideep along with Navi published *The Rise of the Frugal Economy* in 2015 (http://www.project-syndicate.org/commentary/peer-to-peer-economy-by-navi-radjou-1-and-jaideep-prabhu-2015-02). His latest book, *Do Better With Less: Frugal Innovation for Sustainable Growth*, is co-authored with Prof. Navi Radjou (https://penguin.co.in/book/business/do-better-with-less/, published in 2019).

LinkedIn https://www.linkedin.com/in/jaideep-prabhu-94b3102/
Email j.prabhu@jbs.cam.ac.uk

Mr Md Nazmul Huda

Md Nazmul Huda works as a Knowledge Management Specialist at BRAC. In addition, he is a programme analyst in practical action in Bangladesh and has five years of work experience in programme planning, capacity development, business analysis and modelling for different WaSH, urban, livelihoods, agriculture, energy, and humanitarian projects as follows:

✓ developing, upgrading, demonstrating, and putting into practice appropriate technology within communities using participatory approaches;

✓ giving skills training and extending capacity building support to NGO/GO staff;
✓ sharing knowledge and disseminating information and research findings among key stakeholders;
✓ enabling producers and entrepreneurs information and skills for allowing access to market opportunities and linkages;
✓ promoting advocacy and influencing for policy change.

Practical Action's work in Bangladesh has evolved over time to meet the challenges of poverty, inequality, and vulnerability. Deeply committed to helping the poor in Bangladesh, his work on appropriate technology to improve poor people's livelihoods has been flexible and responsive to local conditions and needs.

LinkedIn https://bd.linkedin.com/in/aonik/de
Email me@nazmul-huda.com

Mr Pramod Ratnakar Khadilkar

Pramod Ratnakar Khadilkar is a passionate researcher who believes in a perfect blend of theory and practice in attempting to solve one of the wicked problems on earth, like poverty. Being a designer by education, he feels agonised when design as a profession is only linked with detailing and planning of technical goods without understanding its societal and behavioural dimension. For him *design* is a mode of thinking which is relevant and applicable to any profession and any field of work. He has close to seven years of industry experience with major companies from India. He has a PhD from the Indian Institute of Science, Bangalore. The title of his thesis is 'Methodology to Support Needs Analysis and Behavioural Simulation in Design for Base of the (Economic) Pyramid'. His specialties are design research, design for Base of the Pyramid, application of capability approach to product design, and technical surfacing using alias. Currently, he is working on identifying and operationalising the success indicators for design for behavioural change at the DTU – Technical University of Denmark (Marie-Curie Fellow/EuroTech Postdoc Fellow). Pramod Ratnakar Khadilkar works at the Technical University of Denmark, DTU Management Engineering. A more detailed perspective about design and BOP can be found in his journal paper *Formulating the Design Scope for the Base of the (Economic) Pyramid* (www.mitpressjournals.org/doi/10.1162/DESI_a_00436).

LinkedIn https://in.linkedin.com/in/pramod-khadilkar-99025921
Email prakha@dtu.dk

Dr Lavanian Dorairaj

After retiring in December 2002 from the post of Deputy Director, Medical Services, India Air Force, Wing Commander Dr Lavanian Dorairaj (retd) MBBS began focusing on taking quality based, affordable, and accessible health care to villages. As one of the pioneers in telemedicine and health care informatics, Dr Lavanian has worked with many top organizations, including Apollo hospital groups. In 2009, he formed his own consultancy, HCit Consultant, moving a step closer to achieving his dream. Most of his earnings, in his individual capacity, helped to support the AmbuPod project to the point when the first prototype was rolled out in December 2016. In February 2017 LYNK AmbuPod Pvt. Ltd. was incorporated to exclusively take forward the AmbuPod globally. Thereafter, it moved forward aggressively with its engineering, marketing, and sales activity.

LinkedIn https://www.linkedin.com/in/lavanian/?originalSubdomain=in

The interviews

We started our interviews and investigation with four pivotal questions.

What are the main characteristics of BOP markets and contexts, in particular concerning innovation, business model, network, and challenges?

JAIDEEP PRABHU: First of all, it's very large. There are roughly around three billion people in the world who are in this category. They are mostly operating in the informal economy. They have relatively low income, probably less than $10 a day, and they have unmet needs in every basic area such as financial services, health, education, transport, energy, and so on. Therefore, they often have to resort to informal means; getting access to informal markets means they actually pay a premium for lower quality products. So, this very large market offers companies from the formal economy an opportunity to develop market-based solutions. They have to develop products and services obviously to meet the need but be most affordable, easily available, and accessible to a vast amount of people. It means they have to develop a new business model that can reduce the cost dramatically while being able to counteract by increasing profit from very small margins through greater volume. So this means they have to network and have to work with governments, NGOs, and the communities themselves and co-create and co-deliver.

PRAMOD RATNAKAR KHADILKAR: BOP markets are made-up populations that are sparsely distributed, they lack infrastructure, power, transport, finance, health care, education, etc. The legal mechanisms are weak and the market mostly works on social contracts rather than legal ones. The market is informal in nature. The populations lack basic necessities and thus their choice architecture is not similar to populations with surplus money and matured infrastructure. BOP populations, however, at the same time show so-called irrational behaviour in terms of status consumption. BOP populations at the time are quite skilful at native and living skills in general. Their hand skills are exceptional. They are good problem solvers with limited resources. They have quite a positive outlook towards challenges.

MD NAZMUL HUDA: BOP has a broad definition globally, but locally we usually work with people earning $2.5 a day. Our approach towards such markets is to deliver intermediate technology to such communities to improve their livelihoods. We have implemented participatory market system development (PMSD – a well-experienced and tested version of market systems by practical action) an approach to create agri-producers' network. We have also implemented precise point positioning (PPP) based solutions for city wide solutions. Our major challenge was to finance intermediate technology. Thus, we have introduced subsidised business models into our portfolio, which helped by boosting the performance of the communities we work with.

LAVANIAN DORAIRAJ: My focus is the Indian market. With reference to the Indian market, when we talk about the bottom of the pyramid, there would be two areas: rural and urban areas. In the Indian market, the population in urban areas is around 69% which is twice the number of the population in urban. The urban markets have certain advantages: accessibility is not a problem; however in the rural markets, there is a huge problem here. For example, if the person wants to get medicine in remote areas - even if he has money - there will be problems with accessibility.

There are many challenges in rural areas. These challenges mentioned below are focused on health care:

*   *Accessibility.* AmbuPod has got into this area to help these BOP people, but large companies do not want to get into these areas because of the lack of sustainability from a business perspective. Everybody is looking for profitability. Large companies do not like to get into these areas, because modestly speaking there is no profitability.

- *Lack of manpower.* There are insufficient doctors. There is a shortage of manpower for clinical staff providing health care services. For example, the doctor–patient ratio (average) is around 1:1.700, which is the official ratio in India, but the fact is that most of the doctors stay in cities, and very few qualified doctors desire to practise in rural areas. This results in an actual doctor–patient ratio as bad as 1:60.000.
- *Lack of capability.* A rural person cannot afford continuous health care due to high costs. If you need to provide health care, the baseline should be 60–70 Rupees (nearly $1), which is affordable to those who are BPL (below poverty level).
- *Low level of education.* People in urban areas earn well because of their knowledge. They are able to receive information and process it. For example, people in rural areas often die due to the lack of simple hygiene practices, like washing their hands. Information does not reach them and, even if it does, the significance is not understood or is ignored.
- *Lack of technology.* The internet is an important tool to access information and knowledge via pull or push and, as we know, knowledge is power. The internet also allows remote access to health care via telemedicine services. Regrettably, rural India is still struggling to access internet services. The government is working very hard to get these facilities into rural areas, but there is still a lot to do. If we need to take health care to the remotest of villages then we must resolve this challenge.

How do we resolve these challenges? Not at all easy, if it were, people would have already been doing it. And that's the reason we had to develop an innovative plan, one which would not just take health care to the rural areas but also provide quality based services. The most important requirement is to provide (as in urban areas) 24/7 ambulance services and daily outpatient departments 5 to 6 days per week (up till now, we have, globally, always measured rural health with a different yardstick vis-à-vis urban services. That has to stop, NOW). We started out by ensuring that our plan would provide similar services in rural areas. A big challenge was – how do we do all of this while keeping costs at an affordable level? Especially since bringing urban-like services to the rural environment would (logically) cost more. We resolved the challenge by (a) inventing a special vehicle, the AmbuPod, a low cost micro ambulance, clinic, and telemedicine node all rolled into one; (b) we off-loaded costs by increasingly using telemedicine services to guide locally trained resources, and (c) we evolved algorithms to ensure efficient services from a limited number of doctors by the use of schedules, standard treatment protocols, and triage. The advantage of using locals was that we could provide jobs locally, keep costs low, and since he/she (the local resource) is local, he/she is well aware of local politics, social and cultural barriers, and knows how to resolve them. Our AmbuPod would be fully stocked up and cover a group of villages within a radius of 6 to 10 kilo-metres where it would provide daily OPD (scheduled) services and 24/7 ambulance availability. The cost per service would come to around 60 to 70 Rupees (nearly $1) and most patients would require between 1 to 3 services only. Imagine if these people had gone for treatment to a city that would have cost them a whole day and around 800 to 2000 rupees ($10 to $25).

The other challenge is acquiring funds. This is because (1) ours is a brand new idea with no track record and (2) funders have got used to expecting massive profits thanks to pure IT projects. They are unable to understand a for-profit social business plan that provides profits only when the quantity rises. This is in spite of there being a huge market in health services for remote areas.

Other challenges: There are hundreds of languages in India. Local politics and social norms are another problem. An example is the caste system. In some areas, choosing a low caste educated/intelligent person could be a problem - as higher caste people may reject him.

Which main drivers and barriers do you see in BOP contexts?

JAIDEEP PRABHU: *Drivers*: The main driver in BOP is the share volume of need, so there is a big unmet need to the basic area for a very large number of people which is also increasing. There is a demand. These people know each product and service and what they want. They see that people in the formal economy getting access to these things realise the value of them, and they want them for their children and at least for themselves. So, there is need and demand because they increasingly have some income at their disposal. Many people in BOP have some dispos-able income. And even there is pressure from the government, NGOs, inter-governmental agencies like the UN through sustainable develop-ment goals so there is a general push and pull.
Barriers are the four A's:

- *Awareness*. People in BOP are not aware of possible market solutions that are available and relevant concerning their benefits.
- *Affordability*. It is the big issue. Even if people are aware of them, they may not be able to afford them.
- *Available/access*. Even if people in BOP can afford the above-mentioned benefits, they can't access them because they may not be available especially for those living in remote or rural areas.

- *Acceptable.* Even though they can access them, they can't accept them, because there may be social and cultural barriers.

Sometimes, the government could in a way create barriers by making it more difficult in any of the above mentioned 4 A's. Usually, the government creates a condition for market exchange to transpire, but if the government doesn't create those conditions, then these market exchanges will not happen. First, there needs to be proper infrastructure. If there is no proper physical infrastructure, they can't get access to products and services and it adds to the costs. If there is no infrastructure like telecommunication, they can't attract awareness or get information. So the government often tries to play a positive role, however creates barriers instead. This is on the demand side. On the supply side, the government could create barriers by making it harder for companies to operate, so making it harder for start-ups without making business easier. The regulations may become expensive and harder to operate. I would say the government plays a significant role and there are also barriers within companies, because these are pursuing profit and return on investment. They can always get a higher profit or return on investment with easily accessible segments. So there are barriers with the government and companies.

PRAMOD RATNAKAR KHADILKAR: *Drivers* are

1) The lack of necessities and many unmet needs.
2) Their local skills and resources can be utilised to generate new markets, like rural entrepreneurs harvesting the forest produce etc.

Barriers are

1) Lack of infrastructure.
2) Lack of understanding of rural markets.
3) Lack of planning on the side of businesses; the timelines and resources that are required for a BOP venture is much different than a non-BOP venture. The BOP venture needs a lot of support before and after actual product development in terms of developing support for other life cycle phases like marketing, distribution, service, etc.
4) Two conceptually extreme misunderstandings or gross generalisations – a BOP market is a low hanging fruit, or a BOP market is not suitable for 'for-profit' businesses.

LAVANIAN DORAIRAJ: *Drivers*: Indians are social, caring, and God-fearing. Most have a desire to do good to gain good Karma, and that is a good thing. Secondly, from a commercial perspective, it is a huge market down there, so if you can gain access to the market with the product and sustain/grow for 2–3 years, we will ensure healthy profits. In fact, if we cover 50,000 villages over the next 5 years, we could become a quarter billion US dollar company – and gain lots of good Karma!

Barriers: All the challenges mentioned above are barriers, Difficulty wise I would list them as funding – accessibility – affordability – politics and finally competition.

MD NAZMUL HUDA: Our understanding is that we still require to perform behaviour change communications a lot to help the communities to educate. Lack of knowledge is the key driver preventing entry of products and services into BOP markets. Social exclusion is reducing at a significant rate. But we also have scopes for working for social inclusiveness, too. When people are excluded through social barriers, market systems face difficulties. The BOP communities need strong relationships with political and legal stakeholders. Our socio-cultural context is not so friendly to entrepreneurship and community businesses may become vulnerable without proper networking with the authorities.

How are BOP value co-creation and cross-sector collaboration characterised?

PRAMOD RATNAKAR KHADILKAR: BOP ventures need to look at BOP stakeholders as collaborators and value creators. They are much more knowledgeable regarding context and local challenges. It is well known that the local partner should be involved in venture, however, it is practised from a very narrow view. The local partner is used only as a resource and not as a partner. Using them as a resource has the connotation that they will follow the instructions given; on the other hand taking them as partners change the whole business plan and execution. Cross-sector collaboration is essential because value creation at BOP has to include technology, policy, finance, and governance. As Sen (1999) says in *Development of Freedom*, the government has a role to play and human development is not possible with open markets alone. There is always some aspect of product development which does not give returns in short term where collaboration with the government is necessary. Finance is another important sector which needs some kind of assurance from some legal organization. The BOP stakeholders cannot have access to the finance.

JAIDEEP PRABHU: It is very important to make a business model happen both financially and operationally. Partners are required. Companies need a partner to help them with the 4 A's to create them: awareness, affordability, availability, and acceptability. They have to work with NGOs as they already have an existing relationship with communities that can help to create awareness, affordability, availability, and acceptability. It can help in acceptability, by reducing social and cultural barriers. So it is important and many successful business models will have this element of co-creation and co-delivery even with NGOs, governments, and with the communities themselves (BOP market themselves). Look at micro-finance, people being beneficiary customers, are also part of the solution, part of the business model, because they have a joint liability group, and they actually make a model viable financially and operationally. Look at project Shakti from Unilever, they are trying to deliver products which in most rural areas are affordable. They work with their communities allowing agents that reduce costs, increase affordability, awareness, and acceptability, and so on.

LAVANIAN DORAIRAJ: There are thousands of small and large organizations providing multiple services in rural areas, be it education, women and child care, hygiene, sanitation, drinking water, the girl child, and of course health care. All these groups can actually work together, sharing resources and in the process cut cost of operations, while improving the quality of services and ensuring effectivity at a lower cost. Unfortunately, most organizations are focused on just one vertical, and do not wish to look at collaboration. If there were collaborations, we could do so much more with so much less.

The government of India rules that all organizations making profits must provide 2% of this for social services and calls it CSR (corporate social responsibility). Regrettably many companies use CSR to covertly push their own agenda, rather than any social cause. They are also not willing to cooperate and collaborate since apparently CSR is mostly a drain and effort likewise this has to be kept to a bare minimum. Lastly, such activities are headed by managers who seem to believe in the adage that 'Nothing tried, is nothing lost'. In simple words, we need people with a progressive mindset, people who are willing to open their minds to the fact that we can work together.

MD NAZMUL HUDA: As mentioned, we have devised a participatory market system development approach to build solutions for the BOP markets. We help the communities to cluster based on operating needs at different stages of the value chain. Thus, the cluster specialises at a particular service in the value chain. It helps the businesses to reduce clutter and conflict possibilities. For cross-sector collaborations, we have helped the communities to form network, cooperatives, or service-level agreements for service delivery mechanisms.

What kind of change do you recognise on BOP markets?

LAVANIAN DORAIRAJ: Accessibility has become well, compared to 10 years ago. Availability is also better. Internet availability has grown faster due to the private organizations. The government has come out with a certain innovative scheme to help BOP people. In the last 10 years, there have been definite improvements, but there is still a long way to go, because a lot of these improvements still have to reach remote areas and be functional at least 70% of the time. (I have seen so called 'electrified' villages that only receive power for a few hours a day.)

MD NAZMUL HUDA: Mentioned previously, social exclusion is much reduced although it may require much work to develop from current status, but acceptance of marginal people to mainstream services is well ahead. This progress is not just achieved by us, the corporations wanted to market their products in BOP markets. Micro-financing institutions also played a great role. Our NGO, supported through behaviour change communications, was able to reach this stage in a comprehensive manner.

JAIDEEP PRABHU: First of all, much more formal activities happen, so there are formal companies entering the markets. Some of them also operate as social businesses, so they are not purely out for profit. Often they are the hybrid forms trying to solve the social problems, but at least generating surplus. They may not pay the dividends to their investors. They generate the surplus to cover these costs. We see a lot of formal supply-side activity actually. There are companies and NGOs and social businesses entering the markets. There is much innovation happening. Very interesting products and services as well as business models delivering value - very affordable to a large number of people - can be seen across these sectors. You can see this in the financial services, in telecommunication, health education, energy, food transportation, etc. So, there are lots of activities happening, but the need is so great, the market is still untapped that there is a lot more that can be done. There is a lot of collaboration between state sectors, large companies, NGOs, start-ups, and intergovernmental organizations; there is a lot of collaboration happening. You can also see that it is happening at a different level. Likewise in large regions like Africa, South Africa, and South Asia, etc., you can see this happening at the national level. There are national programmes to achieve this. This is going on at state level, city level, and at many different levels.

PRAMOD RATNAKAR KHADILKAR: It is good that MNCs are realising that it is much more challenging than the list of strategies prescribed by Prahalad (2004) in his seminal book on BOP. BOP challenges are much more operational than conceptual. Conceptually we have understood the challenges quite well, we need to solve the challenges by reflection in action: by being quite flexible in the field and using the theory to adapt the businesses to local challenges. Theory should be used but in a flexible way. A magazine of theories should be made and applied based on contextual challenges. Another important aspect is the inclusion of behavioural aspects in taking business decisions with BOP. The operational knowledge regarding 'understanding the user behaviour and response to an intervention' is missing.

In order to get more detailed knowledge and experience, we asked our interview partners to comment on the following statements:

How would you comment on the following statements?

Sustainability is no issue and not a driver in the context of BOP.

LAVANIAN DORAIRAJ: Sustainability is a major issue, because a lot of projects which have been done decease, due to lack of future-proofing and planning for sustainability.

MD NAZMUL HUDA: Not really. If we do not help a market system to reach sustainability, there will be possibilities for the system to fail in the long run.

PRAMOD RATNAKAR KHADILKAR: Environmental sustainability is never an issue at BOP. They are much more sustainable than the developed world and markets. They are much more resource efficient. However, sustainability is a good way to pitch the businesses for governmental funds. You cannot attract customers to buy the products using environmental sustainability. Financial sustainability is much more than utilitarian approach and needs understanding of the, so-called, irrational behaviour of the stakeholders. Societal and personal sustainability is critical as they are affected by lack of important resources like health care, education, and in general inefficient governance. However, the stakeholders do not understand the importance of these factors and these aspects may not drive the buying decisions yet. However, it is a good buzzword to pitch businesses and attract funds and subsidies.

JAIDEEP PRABHU: I don't fully agree with this statement. To the customers, maybe, sustainability itself is not a top priority. Affordability may be the top priority. For instance, solar lighting and solar energy, customers are not necessarily buying solar energy, because it is sustainable. They will buy it, if it is of better quality, greater reliability, qualitative lighting and it's actually affordable. So, it is not number one for them – nor for the society, governments, or companies. It is important in the long run, because if the solutions are not sustainable, then they are not sustainable from the business or social perspective. For the BOP, sustainability is not the top priority. For the social or business perspective, sustainability is the priority. Sustainability is a driver, but not the major one in the context of BOP.

The sustainable development goals (SDGs) miss BOP markets.

PRAMOD RATNAKAR KHADILKAR: SDGs can be reformulated to any market. SDGs are not market specific, yet I believe they are quite aligned with BOP needs and, thus, markets.

LAVANIAN DORAIRAJ: Sustainability is an idea which applies equally to all markets, be it rural, urban or local. 'Missing' is not appropriate here;

however SDGs are not applied well in rural markets due to the lack of focus, planning, and the mad rush for high profits.

JAIDEEP PRABHU: I don't agree with this statement completely. In fact, the SDGs focus much on BOP and lots of thinking goes on around SDGs that is improving the quality of life in BOP, and they are wide open to market solutions to achieve them.

Sustainability is more a 'western driven concept' than a local or 'home-grown' concept, and, thus, not helpful in the BOP context.

MD NAZMUL HUDA: No, sustainability is rather a global issue. Big businesses survive because they have achieved sustainability. Small businesses have less chances for long-term survival because of sustainable financing, networking, and communication.

LAVANIAN DORAIRAJ: Sustainability is neither foreign nor Indian in concept. It is a basic or global concept which is required for any project. From a BOP perspective, to be able to reach out to the maximum within the BOP, we need to grow and growth will only come when our project first learns to be sustainable. Lack of sustainability spells DEATH to the project.

PRAMOD RATNAKAR KHADILKAR: The use of sustainability as a value proposition for commerce is a western driven concept. Sustainability as a way of living is quite well known to BOP markets. As a concept, sustainability is not well understood. The concept is kept vague to exploit it for the financial purposes by the western world. It is useful at BOP context if the purpose is related to human and social aspects of it. It is a good buzzword to attract funds.

JAIDEEP PRABHU: I would not fully agree with that, I would say, in the western world people may be more aware of sustainability issues, and there might be more issues to consumers' basic needs that are being taking care of. They have the better technician; the economy needs to be sustainable. I think in BOP markets there is more pressure, more immediate pressure from livelihood and survival which means that sustainability may not be the top priority for the consumers, but in the long run it has to be. So, you have to localise the idea of sustainability. For instance, you have to educate or explain the importance of sustainability in terms in order that people can understand their local environment.

BOP markets are mainly about money – social and environmental aspects play a minor role.

PRAMOD RATNAKAR KHADILKAR: Business is essentially about money. Money cannot be ignored. BOP ventures can be much more impactful if they are approached as 'for-profit' financial ventures which can impact social and environmental aspects as well, rather than distributing freebies using aid money. BOP ventures impacting social and environmental aspects can become profitable if planned with a long-term vision.

MD NAZMUL HUDA: To a very minimum companies care about BOP markets for money. But mostly all understanding stakeholders work for BOP markets for social inclusiveness and environmental aspects. It depends on the government policy how approach to a certain market will be drawn.

JAIDEEP PRABHU: I would not agree that they play a role. They play a role, while not a major role, however an important secondary one. Affordability is most common, because if something is not affordable, then there will be simply no market for it. But if it is affordable and not socially acceptable, you won't have a market. If it's affordable, but not environmentally sustainable, then there won't be a market in the long term. So, I think affordability is the main concern, so we also need to think in terms of social and environmental science.

LAVANIAN DORAIRAJ: Regrettable but true. As of to date there is not much concern with social and environmental aspects. Though externally a company may tom-tom about both these aspects, the inside story invariably is to get in make a quick buck, and get out. There are two aspects to this:

- *Private perspective.* I would say, 90% of the people in the private area are (covertly) focused only on profits. Of course there is nothing wrong with that, because if you give a service, you will need to charge for it or it will not sustain. What is bad, is to talk about sustainability while the actual focus is to siphon profits and then get out, and damn the consequences (to the BOP).
- *Government/public perspective.* Different issues here. The officials involved do not really use their minds or care. At the end of the day it is just a job and they would rather not shake the boat, just do the minimum required and get back to the city after completing this 'punishment' tenure. Secondly, many of the projects are done for political gain and self-glorification of that specific government party rather than actually focusing on doing good for the people. Money is also involved here but differently. There are enough stories in the lay press of how crores of rupees are siphoned off in a nexus between contractors, officials, and ministers. And social or environmental aspects be dammed!

Offering goods and services as well as creating value for and with the BOP do not lead to a mitigation of poverty and social exclusion.

LAVANIAN DORAIRAJ: Incorrect, it does. Offering goods and services definitely mitigate difficulties. It also helps improve status, quality of life, and allows merger of the BOP into the mainstream, but it needs to be carefully planned, done in a sustainable way. A lot of planning is required to ensure that it does not convert the BOP into lazy individuals addicted to free hand-outs. They need to be educated, provided purpose and dignity. 'Never give a man a fish, teach him to fish.'

JAIDEEP PRABHU: I totally disagree with this statement. These kinds of innovations, goods and services, create values for the BOP. The whole point is to mitigate poverty and social exclusion. Now here the question would be, what goods and services can you offer them? Maybe, if you offer them a better type of alcohol or tobacco, then it will not necessarily reduce poverty. If you offer them a better way to save money, a better way to get access to a loan, to light their home, cook their food, and educate their children, then I hope it may lead to the reduction of poverty and social exclusion.

PRAMOD RATNAKAR KHADILKAR: I do not agree with this statement. Market is the place where value is exchanged. If one understands the value propositions of BOP market, the BOP stakeholders will surely pay or will get paid.

MD NAZMUL HUDA: I neither agree nor disagree.

BOP markets are dominated by MNCs – SMEs only play a secondary role.

JAIDEEP PRABHU: I don't agree. We are talking about collaboration between MNCs or large domestic companies and SMEs, because the SMEs often have the motivation and local knowledge to come up with initial products or services and business models. They often lack resources to scale, and so they need to look for a bigger partner. Conversely, the big companies have the ability to scale, but often they do not have the motivation to try different things or business models, so there is a good opportunity for partnership. Both play an important role.

PRAMOD RATNAKAR KHADILKAR: I do not agree with this, yet, BOP markets are still informal and local. However, MNCs are becoming more and more important at least in the fast-moving consumer goods markets.

LAVANIAN DORAIRAJ: It is the mix of both. MNCs are doing quite a number of projects from the CSR and commercial perspective. However, if you look at the numbers, those numbers will be mainly large NGO and of course the government. The biggest group is the government that is doing a lot of work in this field.

MD NAZMUL HUDA: In Bangladesh, BOP markets are mostly dominated by micro-financing institutions, then MNCs, and at last NGOs.

Inclusive value creation[1] is mainly a theoretical issue.

MD NAZMUL HUDA: Not at all. We implement these ideas in practice.

JAIDEEP PRABHU: I think it's really a practical issue, and now academics are trying to theorise this.

LAVANIAN DORAIRAJ: It appears to be theoretical, but it should be made practical, it is the only way a country can advance. A country cannot progress unless it cares for the BOP. Any country which has done well has included the poorest of poorest in its economic plans.

PRAMOD RATNAKAR KHADILKAR: It is a conceptual and normative issue. This statement has a connotation as if having theoretical and normative perspective is useless for practice. This is equally harmful for a research and practice fraternity. The real issue is, converting a theory into practice needs additional work, which is missing from both the stakeholders, i.e. academia and practitioners.

BOP markets are dominated by frugal innovations.

JAIDEEP PRABHU: Generally speaking, I agree because you cannot create a market in BOP unless it is affordable, so the innovation has to be frugal. However, some of these frugal innovations exploit expensive innovations. For instance, telecommunication, you see that mobile phones are now everywhere. A lot of frugal innovations provide the use of mobile phones to teach people and enable for reverse services and make them aware of them and so on. So, I would say that the actual business model and innovations are frugal, but are based on innovations that probably require a lot of investment and technology. But generally, I agree with this statement.

PRAMOD RATNAKAR KHADILKAR: Yes, yet it is slowly changing as more and more industrially and mass-produced goods are reaching BOP markets.

MD NAZMUL HUDA: This statement is an indication for the experiments conducted by NGOs to innovate market systems. But actual businesses are not delivering products or services with frugal innovations. You will not find that cow fodder or vegetable markets are established through frugal innovations. There are numbers of existing value chains. The NGOs and development agencies work there to improve the earning and livelihoods of the communities. This does not mean businesses are operating there with frugal innovation.

LAVANIAN DORAIRAJ: Yes, in India at least. Frugal innovation makes the difference because it is perfectly suited to the local environment. The point is that we have a huge population and lack of money/resources is the mother of frugal innovations. And this is making a difference. Now with MNCs coming in with money, many of these frugal innovations can be formalised, quality controlled, and marketed professionally to a larger audience.

Institutional voids and mechanisms are a major barrier to uplifting people at the BOP through business.

JAIDEEP PRABHU: Talking about governmental barriers, sometimes the lack of the institution itself is a barrier. For instance, if you don't have defined regulations or you don't have clarified ways to resolve conflicts or copyright issues, then it can impede the trust in the buyers and sellers. It is hard to create a market. Sometimes, there are governmental institutions or practices that make it hard. So, it's not the void itself, but the presence of institutions. If you have a very conservative banking sector, for instance, then that may be a hindrance and constrain frugal innovations reaching BOP markets. I would say, it's not only the lack of institutions, but sometimes their presence functions as a barrier.

LAVANIAN DORAIRAJ: Regrettably true; for example, our frugal innovation, the first version of the AmbuPod was low-cost and practical but faced insurmountable difficulties in getting certified by government institutions. Government certification organizations have the same yard sticks for frugal innovations when different yardsticks need to be applied. This barrier in the form of rigid rules and regulations makes it impossible for a poor person to take an innovation to the market unless he has tons of money. To quote an example, our AmbuPod chassis costing less than a lakh would require between 15 to 25 lakhs for certification. And that's the reason, frugal can never be defined nor certified whether it is a small tractor made from a lawn mower or some other kind of innovation. Even rules for funding such innovations by the government are red tape bound, complex, slow, impractical, and frequently entwined in corruption through 'agents'.

MD NAZMUL HUDA: To some extent it may be true.

Culture prevents change on BOP markets.

PRAMOD RATNAKAR KHADILKAR: I do not agree with this. Non-BOP will be as irrational and rigid as BOP if faced with resource constraints. These are simplistic generalisations. Abhijeet Banerjee and Esther Duflo (2012) have argued quite effectively against gross generalisations in the book *Poor Economics*.

MD NAZMUL HUDA: The entrants to a BOP market should diversify rather than offering the same service to all markets.

LAVANIAN DORAIRAJ: That depends on the local social environment. The positive thing about an Indian is, that we are open to change and if we see something that is good, we will very easily and positively embrace it. Take the example of mobile phones and smart phones. Many people never thought it would work in rural areas where many are illiterate. Surprisingly people in rural areas have embraced this technology eagerly and India is now one of the countries with the highest density of mobile phones. We are clever, open minded, and ready for change, if the change provides a positive experience. We do not adopt things blindly, just because the government or somebody says so. We weigh its pros and cons and if positive, embrace it very quickly.

JAIDEEP PRABHU: Yeah, but it's a quite broad statement, because culture can work on the national level, society one or government, large or all companies. There is, of course, the cultural customer. In general, culture can prevent change, so the consumers in BOP may be conservative. The consumers may be a part of a very conservative social or cultural context, which makes it hard for them to change or adopt a change in behaviour. However, there also may be a lot of conserved culture in companies and government due to which they don't try out new things, or reach to new markets or encourage innovations. So, the existing culture can be a barrier, but then the question will be how can you make cultural changes? One of the reason is that SMEs can respond better here, because they have a generally proactive culture or entrepreneurial culture, they are willing to try out new things. SMEs are willing to perceive the changing of the culture of customers whereas bigger companies remain conservative and governments tends to be conservative as well. Culture depends on what they are talking about, it acts as a barrier as well. Potentially if culture alters, change can happen.

Note

1 According to UNDP (2010, p. 18), inclusive strategies build bridges and imbed poor or BOP people 'on the demand side as clients and customers and on the supply side as employees, producers and business owners at various points along value chains'.

References

Arnold, M. (2018) Sustainability value creation in frugal contexts to foster sustainable development goals. *Business Strategy and Development, 1(4), Special Issue: The role of SDGs for progressing sustainability,* 265–275, https://doi.org/10.1002/bsd2.36.

Banerjee, A. V., & Duflo, E. (2012). *Poor Economics: A Radical Rethinking of the Way to Fight Global Poverty* (paperback first published). New York: PublicAffairs.

Brem, A., & Wolfram, P. (2014). Research and development from the bottom up – introduction of terminologies for new product development in emerging markets. *Journal of Technology Management for Growing Economies, 3(1),* 9.

Govindarajan, V., & Ramamurti, R. (2011). Reverse innovation, emerging markets, and global strategy. *Global Strategy Journal, 1*(3–4), 191–205.

Jagtap, S., Larsson, A., Hiort, V., Olander, E., Warell, A., & Khadilkar, P. (2014). How design process for the Base of the Pyramid differs from that for the Top of the Pyramid. *Design Studies, 35*(5), 527–558.

Papaioannou, T. (2014). How inclusive can innovation and development be in the twenty-first century? *Innovation and Development, 4*(2), 187–202.

Prahalad, C. K. (2004). *The Fortune at the Bottom of the Pyramid: Eradicating Poverty Through Profits.* New Jersey: Wharton School Publishing.

Prahalad, C. K., & Hammond, A. (2002). Serving the world's poor, profitably. *Harvard Business Review, 80*(9), 48–59.

Rosca, E., Arnold, M., & Bendul, J. (2016). Business models for sustainable innovation. An empirical analysis of frugal products and services. *Journal of Cleaner Production*, 126, 133–145. https://doi.org/10.1016/j.jclepro.2016.02.050

Sen, A. (1999). *Development as Freedom*. Oxford: OUP.

Shivarajan, S., & Srinivasan, S. (2013). The poor as suppliers of intellectual property: a social network approach to sustainable poverty alleviation. *Business Ethics Quarterly*, 23(3), 381–406.

Silvestre B. S., & Silva Neto, R. 2014. Capability accumulation, innovation, and diffusion: lessons from a Base of the Pyramid cluster. *Technovation 34*, 270–283.

Simanis, E., & Hart, S. L. (2008). *The Base of the Pyramid Protocol: Toward Next Generation BOP Strategy* (second edn). Ithaca, New York: Center for Sustainable Global Enterprise, Cornell University.

Soni, P., & Krishnan, R. T. (2014). Frugal innovation: aligning theory, practice, and public policy. *Journal of Indian Business Research*, 6(1), 29–47.

UNDP (2010). *Inclusive Market Development. Brokering Inclusive Business Models*. Retrieved from http://www.undp.org/content/dam/undp/library/corporate/Partnerships/Private%20Sector/Brokering%20Inclusive%20Business%20Models.pdf

Webb, J. W., Kistruck, G. M., Ireland, R. D., & Ketchen, D. J. (2010). The entrepreneurship process in Base of the Pyramid markets: the case of multinational enterprise/nongovernment organization alliances. *Entrepreneurship Theory and Practice, 34*(3), 555–581.

Zeschky, M. B., Winterhalter, S., & Gassmann, O. (2014). From cost to frugal and reverse innovation: mapping the field and implications for global competitiveness. *Research-Technology Management, 57*(4), 20–27.

2 Benefits of cross-border collaboration at Base of the Pyramid markets for innovation improvement

Usama Awan, Nazia Suleman, Janne Huiskonen, and Andrzej Kraslawski

Introduction

In recent years, export manufacturing firms from developing countries have been confronted with challenges of innovation and sustainable development to contribute positively to the United Nations Sustainable Development Goals (SDGs). The developing countries which are characterised by labour-intensive and mass means of production are expected to continue to face challenges of affordable and reliable means of income and quality of living standards. Particularly, for lower-income countries, innovation and infrastructure development is crucial in achieving sustainable development and empowering communities. The SDGs represent a set of 17 priorities for global development that focuses on environmental, social, and economic dimensions with a total of 169 targets. Among the 17 SDGs, goal 9 is 'build infrastructure, promote sustainable industrialisation and foster innovation' in developing countries. Cleaner production technologies and industrial process are of a wide significance for developed as well as developing countries (United Nations Statistical Commission, 2017). Among the nine targets of SDG 9, target 9.3 and 9.4 are aimed at upgrading technological capabilities to make them sustainable, with greater adoption of cleaner production technologies and encouraging innovation in developing countries. This requires attention because the up-gradation of technological infrastructure enhances research and development activities primarily have an impact on innovation. The least developed countries often do not have sufficient resources to promote sustainable industrialisation and foster innovation. Following the seminal paper by Prahalad and Hart (2002), the Bottom of Pyramid (BOP) concept is based on the idea that poverty can be alleviated through 'providing prospective rewards [which] include[s] growth, profits and incalculable contributions to humankin' (Prahalad & Hart 2002, p. 1). Base or bottom of pyramid terms are used interchangeably in literature to represent the population which is less economically privileged, constituting more than 4 billion people living on less than \$2 per day while proposed earning lies between \$1000 to \$2000. Some scholars use a threshold of \$1 to \$2 (Kolk, Rivera-Santos, & Rufín, 2014).

The human development issues, in the beginning, have been discussed in BOP literature, for example by Prahalad and Hart (2002). These standards on human development in the workplace play a vital role in upgrading products and process. Human development has been discussed in the BOP literature from the very beginning (see, for example, (Prahalad & Hart, 2002). Add to this the idea that collaboration is a strategic opportunity for companies that wish to achieve sustainable development and both researchers and practitioners need to understand the important relationships impacting innovation (Chen et al., 2017). The collaborations refer to working jointly with the partners (Large & Thomsen, 2011).

Promoting innovation in BOP markets becomes an inevitable strategy. Awan, Kraslawski, and Huiskonen (2018b) revealed that collaboration fosters the configuration of resources that allow partners to improve operational competencies. This cooperation depends on repeated communication and understanding of practical experience held by partner firms (Lakemond, Bengtsson, Laursen, & Tell, 2016). We, therefore, believe that collaboration will indeed help to manage relationships between firms in the context of sustainability (Niesten, Jolink, de Sousa Jabbour, Chappin, & Lozano, 2017). As Awan et al. (2018b) demonstrate, collaboration is necessary for the development of the infrastructure as well as compliance with the policies on occupation health and labour standards. According to Awan, Kraslawski, and Huiskonen (2018c), a positive association exists between social performance improvement and innovation. Despite this comprehension, there remains a gap in our understanding of how organizational learning and dynamic capability perspective enabling can happen through internal communication (Benner, 2009; Pavlou & El Sawy, 2011; Piening & Salge, 2015). Given the relevance of cooperation, some fresh research studies have started to deal with inter-firm relationship aiming to achieve sustainability objectives (Govindan, Seuring, Zhu, & Azevedo, 2016). Grekova et al. (2016) found that collaboration involving environmental performance with suppliers influences a firm's performance. Awan, Muneer, and Abbas (2013) have described the collaborative organizational culture aimed at encouraging innovation.

Previous research has reported a significant association between collaboration and social performance (Awan et al., 2018b; Luzzini, Brandon-Jones, Brandon-Jones, & Spina, 2015; Sancha, Wong, & Thomsen, 2016) and between environmental collaboration and innovation performance (Macchion et al., 2017). However, we have found there has been little research on the impact of collaboration on a firm's innovation performance. Research by Gimenez, Sierra, and Rodon (2012) provides some mixed results regarding collaboration on sustainability initiatives and the triple bottom line (TBL) performance. The existing research studies revealed that a firm's innovation takes place in the environment provided by the market place wherein businesses operated (Tavassoli, 2015).

BOP related research has gained increasing attention in recent years. The global firms have the potential to help in creating and developing markets for innovations (Palomares-Aguirre, Barnett, Layrisse, & Husted, 2018). There is little understanding of how firms pursuing sustainability initiatives operationalise these opportunities and how this, in turn, influences innovation. We found that there is a gap in prior research that has not yet provided insights as to the mechanisms through which collaboration affects firm-level innovation. The mixed empirical results to date suggest that intervening variables might provide a better understanding of the strength and direction of relationships It is important to explore this line of research to understand what else can enhance firm-level innovation. Little research to date tests whether a firm's operational capacities explain performance along dimensions of innovation. Within the globalisation and a changing manufacturing landscape, insightful research opportunities are now coming from developing economies. To this end, Pakistan is a new and compelling case for studying developing innovation and operational capacities within manufacturing firms. For that reason, there is also a compulsion to establish creative business practices and innovative solutions and information, which can be designed to the BOP business context making it possible for firms to execute effectively in developing markets and play an important role in the development of social well-being of individual and society (Schuster & Holtbrügge, 2012).

There is a need for research investigating the impact of collaboration on innovation performance outcomes. The empirical validation of business management practices will help advance item measurement, construct development, and give new insights into a dynamic relationship involving sustainability initiatives, social performance, and innovation. This study empirically investigates how collaboration can be used to influence social performance improvement, which, in turn, leads to improve innovation performance. The central aim of our study is to answer the research question how and why cross-border collaboration framed as a resource can trigger innovation performance of export manufacturing firms in the developing country.

We focused on these export manufacturing firms because of their contribution to the Pakistan economy and their experience in dealing with their international clients/customers. The Faisalabad and Sialkot exports earnt approximately $3.26 billion, nearly 56% of the gross domestic production (GDP) of Pakistan in 2014–2015. The study includes export manufacturing firms from different industries. The sample list was based on the 2009 list of export manufacturers that were registered in the Sialkot Chamber of commerce and Faisalabad Chamber of Commerce. The data was collected through a self-administered questionnaire-based survey from the target respondents. Thus, to reduce the common method bias, we use co-variance base structural equation modelling in the availability of small sample sizes.

This chapter contributes to the literature in two ways. First, this study contributes to the growing study of innovation literature by developing and testing the different effects of both collaboration and social performance improvements on innovation. Second, this study is among the first to focus on an analysis of social performance improvements, which affects innovation performance. Moreover, export manufacturing firms from the Base of the Pyramid (BOP) need to position their collaboration at social and environ- mental related issues and need to improve social performance.

Synthesis of the Base of the Pyramid

The Base of the Pyramid (BOP) concept is based on the 'understanding of the consumption and expenditure patterns of the poor, as well as of the market structures that characterize their environment' (Kolk et al., 2014, p. 16). Many companies have taken a greater interest in BOP markets as a laboratory of innovation due to rapid changes in the global business en- vironment not just serving an existing market but also for the established country markets (Prahalad, Di Benedetto, & Nakata, 2012). In accordance with a report of ten innovation process documented in the United Nations development programme (2008), innovation for BOP has a tendency to in- clude customers at the latter part of the product development stage (Belz & Krämer, 2008). To this bottom line, the BOP studies state that organiza- tions need to find out about the requirements of low-income focus markets, as well as employing a user-oriented model (London & Hart, 2010). The composition of BOP also depends on the relative size of income and afforda- bility to buy goods. Many BOP markets are mainly concentrated within South-East Asia, Africa, and Latin America (Kistruck & Beamish, 2010). In recent times, the BOP market is more especially associated with organiza- tional sustainability and CSR activities (Arnold & Valentin, 2013; Tarafdar, Anekal, & Singh, 2012).

Earnings are the basic common unit through which individuals are cate- gorised as part of BOP (Subrahmanyan & Tomas Gomez-Arias, 2008). Fur- ther, they estimated that the 4 billion poorest in the world were in the lower level of the economic pyramid; that is, at the bottom or base of the pyramid (Prahalad & Hammond, 2002). Prahalad et al. (2012) suggest that for inno- vation to be achieved a firm must have an understanding of the dynamics of these markets and the process of innovation. The one way to support the BOP population is by finding creative ways of collaboration with their part- ners on environmental issues. Inter-organizational collaboration is a unique way to implement policies and practices for health and safety improvements. Previous research made some concentrated effort to combine concepts of the sustainable supply chain and the BOP in international business perspective (Gold, Hahn, & Seuring, 2013). One of the important aspects of BOP is to engage with a supplier to ensure that they use their resources in the best in- terest of companies (Rivera-Santos & Rufín, 2010).

The cooperation between the local and international partners resulted in the development and improvement in working conditions and a good salary. In accordance with the World Resource Institute, BOP markets comprise of individuals who have the average annual earnings of $3,000, scaled to

2002 US dollars (Webb, Kistruck, Ireland, & Ketchen, 2010). The traditional worker's monthly salary was minimum $US 100. Now employees are earning about $US 160 monthly (Tribune, 2014). On the other hand, in Sialkot, manufacturers of sports goods revealed that purchase orders received by Pakistan decreased in the last decade (The Economic Times, 2018). The sports manufacturing firms in Pakistan is just an example where the older generations have retired from factories and the younger generation is not ready to work in the stitching units. The South Asian regions, in particular Pakistan, remains famous for producing quality sports balls. Pakistan-made footballs were used in the FIFA 2018 World Cup matches (*The Economic Times*, 2018). The BOP population which worked in the sports manufacturing firms had to work in minimum labour standards with no job security. The working conditions in the manufacturing sectors are improving, but largely remain at the bottom. This is consistent with the concepts of collaboration and co-ordination promoted by the BOP theory (Schuster & Holtbrügge, 2014). Collaboration is considered a cornerstone of the goals of sustainable development (Pagell & Wu, 2009). Although BOP research has been part of international relationship management (Gold et al., 2013; Khalid et al., 2015), the development of a long-term relationship with various stakeholders is one of the key BOP strategies (Ramani & Mukherjee, 2014).

Social performance

The Brundtland Report in 1987 provides a triple bottom line framework for measuring the performance of the business in three sustainability dimensions: economic, environmental, and social. The report defined the term as the 'development that meets the needs of the present generations without compromising the ability of future generations to meet their own needs' (WCED, 1987, p. 47). The social line of the triple bottom line framework refers to the impact of organizational fair business practices on human capital, labour, and community (Elkington, 1997). It pertains to the capability of an organization to identify the practices which have an impact on individuals and society in order to support future generations. The World Commission on Environment and Development's (WCED, 1987), broad definition of sustainable development is widely accepted as recognising the importance and integration of social, environmental, and economic performance. The social performance is a component of the triple bottom line (Kleindorfer, Singhal, & Van Wassenhove, 2005). The idea of social performance has been defined by a corporate social responsibility (CSR) perspective (Wood, 1991). Following this point of view, the existing literature on social performance is diverse. Some scholars define it as follows: an 'equal opportunity principle should be understood as an inherent part of the concept of sustainable development, both within and between generations' (Lafferty & Langhelle, 1999, p. 23). On the other side, for example, Carter and Jennings (2002) enumerate social dimensions, such as safety and human rights, diversity, and philanthropy.

The most important channels of the discussion that have come about to deal with additional ways to poverty elimination are the BOP strategies and include market views (Halme et al., 2016). These scholars, as well as business practitioners, have recently got growing concentration on low-income markets in developing and emerging markets (Kolk et al., 2014). Social performance is becoming more important for all companies and is a vital dimension of corporate performance (Nunes, Alamino, Shaw, & Bennett, 2016). The social performance aims to focus on existing business practices and its growth for the upcoming generation in fairness and a judicious manner (Awan, Kraslawski, & Huiskonen, 2018a). If performance improvements in health and safety, human rights, and gender equality are significant, the company can attain more social sustainability. The social sustainability aspects of a manufacturing firm supply chain are of particular concern because this deals with the management of human and societal capital (Sarkis, Helms, & Hervani, 2010). The social issues in the supply chain such as health and safety, bonded child labour, and worker job environment have an impact on a firm's social performance (Hutchins & Sutherland, 2008). The social performance aims to have value for the existing and future generations (Awan, 2017).

Hypothesis development

Firms which collaborate with their customers have the option to collect the knowledge skills and tasks of a business process. These practices have a significant influence on social performance improvements. Collaboration has a positive and direct effect on a firm's social performance (Sancha, Gimenez, & Sierra, 2016). According to Awan et al. (2018b), collaboration has the central function of sharing information and transfer knowledge. They suggest that collaboration is a way to improve social performance. The social performance improvement in a supply chain incorporates health and safety issues and improvement of environmental issues (Ehrgott, Reimann, Kaufmann, & Carter, 2011). The socially sustainable performance dimensions incorporate health and safety issues, improvement of environmental issues, and child labour (Linton et al. 2007; Seuring & Muller 2008; Carter & Easton 2012). More recently, Chen et al. (2017) and Esfahbodi, Zhang, Watson, and Zhang (2017) found a significant positive direct effect of collaboration and sustainability performance. The social performance improvement gained through collaboration may depend on the firm's stock of resources and knowledge. Recent literature suggests that social and environmental collaboration shape innovation performance improvements in developing economies (Awan & Sroufe, 2020).

Moreover, Gimenez et al. (2016) suggest that firms can achieve better results through collaboration. Further, Awan (2019) finds that joint planning and cooperation is linked to an improvement in social performance. As knowledge and resources are drawn from multiple customers, they have a greater impact on a firm's social performance. Because of this, collaboration improves knowledge resources, which is critical for developing a new process. We posit that given collaborations with and working in a greater number of customers will develop a greater domain of specific knowledge aimed at leverage resources to improve social performance. This means, in collaboration, firms have to undergo multiple accommodation processes. As a result, collaboration results in better accommodation of preventive measures at the firm's level, which improves labour standards and policies on safety and security. Three hypotheses are introduced below and outlined in Figure 2.1.

Hypothesis 1: Collaboration has a positive relationship with social performance improvements

Social performance improvement is set to be one of the biggest trends of the next decades, promising a reduction in industrial incidents, improvement of the safety and security of employees, and improvement of employment and labour standards (Awan & Sroufe, 2020). Social performance improvements are about the wellbeing of human beings. Scholars argue that employees are an important player and the primary source for the firm's success and competitive advantage (Barney, Ketchen, & Wright, 2011). Equally, improvements in buyer innovation performance through collaborative buyer-supplier relationships are increasingly critical to improvements in product design, process design, ability to innovate, and shorter product development times. We argue that such links exist because of the presence of a safe working environment and a firm's compliance with occupational and health practices affects the firm's performance. The literature has revealed the collaboration effect of strategic change; it leads to the generation of ideas, reduction of cost, and improvement in product quality (Carey, Lawson, & Krause, 2011).

Moreover, Liu, Zhu, and Yang (2010) argue that employees' motivation can be boosted by creating conditions for workers' participation in joint decision making and encourage group work and promote productivity. This satisfaction may facilitate the process and product innovation by acquiring insights into best practices and the deeper specific knowledge required for product innovation. A supportive work environment for employee comfort, health, and safety increases work engagement that results in enhanced creative performance (Dul & Ceylan, 2011). The importance of improvements in health and safety, environmental conditions, and compliance with the code of conduct shows that these improvements go hand in hand with improvements in the design of new processes and products. Moreover, Liu et al. (2010) argue that creating conditions for employees to participate in joint decision making and encouraging group work boosts employee motivation, and, in turn, increases productivity. According to Awan et al. (2018c), improvement in social performance is positively associated with improvements in innovation performance. In the literature, we found that most social performance improvement in firms will lead to better firm innovation performance improvements. As discussed earlier, the presence of a safe working environment and firm compliance with occupational and health practices encourage group work to participate in joint decision making. Thus we suggest that,

Hypothesis 2: Social performance improvements have a positive relationship with innovation performance improvements

Previous studies have explored the relationships between collaboration and a firm's performance (Cao & Zhang, 2011; Schoenherr & Swink, 2012). Previous literature provides support for the need for collaboration during product and process quality improvements (Macchion et al., 2017; Seuring & Muller, 2008; Vachon & Klassen, 2008). Also, Grekova et al. (2016) found that collaboration with customers has a positive impact on supplier process improvements. Social performance literature increasingly addresses concerns about green innovation resulting from collaborative organizational activities (Awan, Sroufe, & Kraslawski, 2019). Similarly, Gkypali, Filiou, and Tsekouras (2017) suggest that collaboration diversity is negatively associated with innovation performance improvement. Laursen and Salter (2014) found that the collaboration relationship had a positive effect on innovation performance.

Based on the literature, we suggest that by increasing external collaboration on a social issue, firms can assess resources they would lack otherwise. However, such firm-level benefits should be available; they have the appropriate type and level of absorptive capability. According to the knowledge-based view, the development of knowledge capabilities may lead to the development of new process and products. The knowledge-based view involves the transformation of inputs into outputs for the development of new products and process and improves a firm's performance (Grant, 1996). Collaboration is most important for pursuing shared opportunities to be open to solve problems jointly and to renew resources and skills (Lusch & Vargo, 2014). Conceptually, the knowledge-based view assumes that knowledge resources are the outcome of exchange information, where both partners share appropriate knowledge, and decide what is important and weigh the potential cost and benefits.

The study by Un and Asakawa (2015) suggests that collaboration help firms achieve innovation process outcomes. Innovation process consists of tacit and internal proponents (Pisano & Shih, 2012). This, in turn, boosts employee satisfaction. Following this stream of logic, we suggest that firm efforts to incorporate social performance improvement and sustainability initiatives will help to develop new process and introduce new products. Previous work has yet to find a direct link between collaboration and innovation performance improvements. Thus, we propose that:

Hypothesis 3: Collaboration has a positive relationship with innovation performance improvements.

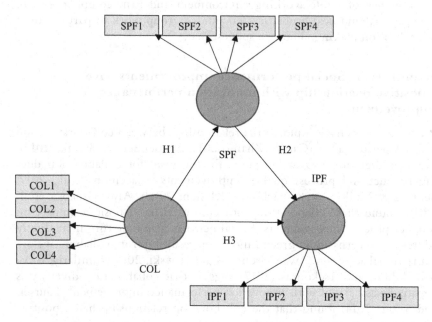

Figure 2.1 Conceptual model

Data methodology

Research in context

The empirical context for the study sets a population parameter of export manufacturing firms in Pakistan. We focused on these export manufacturing firms because of their contribution to the Pakistan economy and their experience in dealing with their international clients/customers. We chose the export manufacturing firm as the stimulus because export manufacturing firms often use collaboration to improve innovation performance (Awan, 2017). Pakistan is a global production base of textile, sports goods, and surgical instruments, exporting a wide variety of goods to Europe and Western countries (Awan & Sroufe, 2020).

Constructs and measures

We selected the construct and measures for independent and dependent variables from the existing literature. Based on prior studies (Vachon & Klassen, 2008), we measured collaboration using four items reflecting the extent of cooperation among functions. The social performance constructs adopted were conceptualised as a reflective contract (Awaysheh & Klassen, 2010; Kleindorfer, Singhal, & Van Wassenhove, 2005). Respondents were asked to consider the extent to which they had improved social performance through collaboration with their customers over the last three years. Innovation performance was measured using established scales adapted from Kotabe, Martin, and Domoto (2003). Respondents were asked to indicate the degree to which they had improve the innovation performance, over the three years. Questionnaires were constructed in English, and a pilot test was carried out among the 11 senior managers from the export manufacturing firms. The export firms in Pakistan mainly use the English language with their counterparts. We drew all the measured items and scales from the prior research studies (see Appendix A).

Sample and data collection

We obtained our sample firms from the registered list of exporters maintained by the federal chamber of commerce and industry. Survey data were collected onsite from the manufacturing firms in Sialkot and Faisalabad from March to April 2017. For this, we identified 650 export manufacturing firms as the sampling frame. The focus on the export manufacturing firms was based on several factors: (i) significant contribution to Pakistan economy and (ii) evidence of learning from their foreign customers and significant export domain to developed countries (Awan, Khattak, & Kraslawski, 2019). A questionnaire was administered to the managers of these sampling firms. In total, we obtained 186 questionnaires in the first three weeks. We then followed this with telephone calls and through sending them an email, and a total of 71 responses were received after the three weeks. Following data collection of two months, responses were received from 257 firms, of which 148 were found to be unusable due to missing values or had a large portion of incomplete data. A list of all the constructs and measurement items is provided in Appendix (A). Table 2.1 shows the validation of the constructed survey items.

We used an independent sample t-test to check for non-response bias with the data. The common method variance (CMV) bias was tested using the unrotated factor analysis extracted method to establish whether CMV is a problem for the data or not. CMV arises when data from the independent and dependent variable is collected at the same time from single respondents by employing a single survey instrument (Podsakoff & Organ, 1986). We used Harmon's single factor test to assess the potential of CMV on collected data as suggested and followed the procedures described in Podsakoff, MacKenzie, Lee, and Podsakoff (2003). A total number of three factors emerged with a total variance explained of 28.03%. This revealed that CMV was not an issue for this data (Reinartz, Haenlein, & Henseler, 2009). The early and late respondents/informants were compared for group difference using the t-test statistics (Armstrong & Overton, 1977).

Results

To test the hypothesis, the data analyses were conducted by using IBM SPSS Statistics and partial least square (PLS) structural equation modelling. We preferred PLS mainly because it illustrates much better convergence patterns, as compared to co-variance base structural equation modelling in the availability of small sample sizes. It concentrates on the prediction of the endogenous variable (Henseler, Hubona, & Ray, 2016). We analysed the suggested structural model according to the indicator, importance, and significance of the structural paths, R-square, and Q^2 redundancy test for predictive relevance (Nitzl, Roldan, & Cepeda, 2016). Standardise root mean square (SRMR) has become an important criterion to assess the root mean square difference between the model–implied correlations and correlations observed for the composite factor model (Henseler, Ringle, & Sarstedt, 2015).

In order to obtain a good measurement model, factor loadings coefficients of all measures were above 0.5, construct reliabilities exceed 0.70, and scores of AVE ranging from 0.56 to 0.84 above the variance due to the measurement error. The result shows that convergent validity has been established for all three measures. Results of the discriminant and convergent validity are presented in Table 2.2. Cronbach's alpha coefficient value of all variables exceeded the recommended cut-off point; all values ranged from 0.77 to 0.93, supporting the reliability of the scale (Nunnally & Bernstein, 1994). In analysing the measurement model, we followed the procedure suggested by Hair and Hult (2016) for identification of model misspecification. We examined the coefficient of determination (R^2), and standardised root means square residual (Henseler et al., 2014). The results show the scores of the

Table 2.1 Validation of the constructed survey items

Items	Factor loadings a	t-value
Innovation Performance Improvement (IPF)		
IPF 1	0.722	17.164
IPF 2	0.852	40.477
IPF 3	0.805	30.168
IPF 4	0.713	12.560
Social Performance (SPF)		
SPF1	0.774	19.547
SPF2	0.864	30.583
SPF3	0.840	35.746
SPF4	0.734	13.170
Collaboration (COL)		
COL 1	0.666	12.539
COL 2	0.821	34.428
COL 3	0.786	25.036
COL 4	0.755	19.441

factors were all above the cut-off value of 0.70 and, thus, significant (Hair & Hult, 2016). It is also clear from the resulting output of factor analysis that all items load with their related construct; this shows that the study had an adequate level of convergent validity. Average Variance Extraction (AVE) achieves the acceptable standard and the score was greater than 0.5. Further, all factors scores reliabilities met the standard cut-off point of 0.60, which support that measures had convergent validity (Bagozzi & Yi, 1988). Convergent validity was assessed using the criteria suggested by Fornell and Larcker (1981).

Blindfolding is a statistical method which is widely used for assessing the predictive strength of the structural equation models (Hair & Hult, 2016). The effect size f^2 (Cohen, 1992) and cross-validated redundancy index (Q^2) (Chin, 1998) results are presented in Table 2.3. The effect size f^2 was also examined for the interaction effect. The value of 0.02 implies that the effect size is small, 0.15 implies that the effect size is medium, and 0.35 indicates that the effect size is high.

The results of path coefficient analysis from PLS-SEM is shown in Table 2.4. The results of the first hypothesis show that collaboration positively influenced social performance ($\beta=0.321$, $t=4.83$), supporting hypothesis 1. This suggests that collaboration is a useful solution for improving social performance. As predicted in hypothesis 2, the path from the social

Table 2.2 Reliability and validity results

	Average variance extraction (AVE)	Composite reliability (CR)	Cronbach's alpha (CA)
IPF	0.601	0.857	0.778
SPF	0.648	0.880	0.819
COL	0.578	0.844	0.753

IPF: innovation performance improvement; SPF: social sustainability performance; COL: collaboration

Table 2.3 f^2 and Q^2 result output

f^2 -results

	Original sample	T-statistics
SPF -> IPF	0.108	2.095
COL-> IPF	0.114	2.072
COL -> SPF	0.204	2.317
Stone–Geisser's test (Q^2) statistic results		
IPF	0.132	–
SPF	0.095	–
IPF=R^2 =0.250; SPF=R^2 =0.170		

SRMR: Standardized root mean square residual: 0.0582
Effect size: f^2 and q^2 0.02 =Small, 0.15 = Medium 0.35 = Large.

Table 2.4 PLS path coefficient results

Path directions	Coefficient	T-statistics
COL -> SPF	b = 0.321	4.833
SPF -> IPF	b = 0.412	6.023
COL -> IPF	b = 0.320	10.14

performance improvements impacted innovation performance positively (β=0.412, t=6.02). This indicates that social performance improvement can be affected by firms' efforts to improve innovation performance. As suggested in hypothesis 3, the path from collaboration and innovation performance was significant (β=0.320, t=10.14). Thus hypothesis 3 is supported. Figure 2.2 shows the model and PLS-SEM results.

An important finding is that social performance affects collaboration and innovation performance improvements. The finding reveals that the manufacturing sector in Pakistan requires a high level of social performance improvements. This requirement can compel a firm to engage in collaboration with its external supply chain partners. The process of knowledge creation through collaboration paves the way for social performance towards the greater innovation performance improvements. These results can help inform other manufacturing firms in developing economies to enable social sustainability, collaboration, and innovation.

Discussion

This study attempts to offer insights into the effect of collaboration on innovation performance improvements. The study is in line with the United Nations Sustainable Development Goal 9, which highlights the need for infrastructure development for innovation in developing countries through enhanced collaboration. Our findings suggest that collaboration influences can significantly affect the improvements in product and process innovation. Firstly, this study contributes to the literature on innovation. The present study responded to a research call from Hull and Rothenberg (2008) by examining the effects of corporate social performance on firm innovation with a focus on internal innovation. In this study, we establish a link between social performance and innovation performance. This research extends this line of research which states that firm-specific home country resources are not enough to facilitate innovation performance improvement. Our study proposes that external collaboration is an essential drive for a firm's social performance improvement. There is a growing recognition of the importance of collaborative efforts in boosting a firm's innovation performance (Gkypali et al., 2017). More specifically, we explore how sustainability orientation and network relationships can further influence an emerging market manufacturing firm's social performance improvements.

Secondly, this study contributes by demonstrating how social performance improvements shape the relationship between collaboration and innovation performance improvements. This study makes empirical and theoretical contributions. The chapter contributes to the sustainability literature on social performance, which has already been studied in developed countries (Huq, Stevenson, & Zorzini, 2014; Yawar & Seuring, 2017). We argue that collaboration on social and environmental issues contributes to explaining the social performance improvements from manufacturing firms within an emerging economy perspective. The results provided evidence on how collaboration affects social performance. By improving social performance, BOP markets firms would be able to retain workers, and ongoing collaboration with their external partners could lead to adoption and upgrading technologies and affect the purchase orders. Staying away from the collaboration could deprive BOP markets of a purchase order (*The Economic Times*, 2018). Our results have highlighted how the collaboration choice of a BOP markets firm can help firms also mitigate the risk of higher orders from their international partners.

This study extends this line of research to explore how different types of sustainability and network relationships might further influence emerging market manufacturing firms and their social performance improvements. This study contributes to the theoretical base of the strategic management literature. The use of the knowledge-based view to frame empirical insights provides theoretical contributions, as it advances the understanding of how inter-organizational collaboration influences the social performance improvements in BOP markets. It provides empirical support for the knowledge-based view that firms with superior knowledge resources can align external knowledge resources and later leads to the development of resources through these collaborations. Thus our findings are in line with Schuster and Holtbrügge (2014), who points out that if companies rely on beneficial resources and knowledge to gain social and innovation performance outcomes, it enables companies to respond to the different challenges of BOP markets.

This study extends our knowledge of innovation performance in manufacturing firms in various ways. Firstly, building on the knowledge-based view, we theoretically establish the specific resources and collaboration which may help the firms in improving social performance, provided that they are overly dependent on the knowledge transfer activities from external stakeholders. Secondly, we empirically identified that improvement in social performance could be achieved by integrating resources and compliance with the regulations on policies, and improvement in health and safety issues. We also found evidence that manufacturing firms in South Asian countries do have the potential to improve their social sustainability if they leverage their resources and capabilities. Such conditions are beneficial to pursue innovation performance. The results highlight that by focusing on social performance improvements, companies gain a better understanding of the conditions under which practices

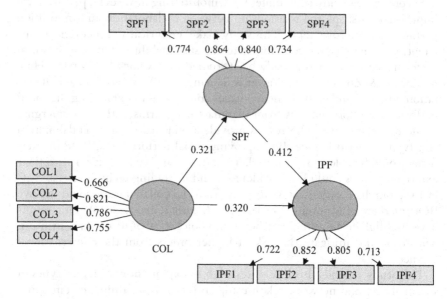

Figure 2.2 PLS path model and results

are determinants of innovation performance improvements. Previous results have shown a positive association between environmental sustainability and innovation performance improvements (Macchion et al., 2017).

Empirically, this study enhances the understanding of how collaboration and social performance shape the innovation performance improvements in the manufacturing industry in emerging economies. In line with the suggestions of Haanaes et al. (2011), sustainability practices are essential for future business landscape. The findings confirm our conceptual model, in that suppliers need to investigate more dynamics of collaboration to develop specialised knowledge. This study suggests that where institutional or legal guarantees are lacking, collaboration becomes an assurance to create an improved sustainability performance. This finding is also in line with Husted and Sousa-Filho (2017). We argue that BOP markets firms are focused on the western firms creating a collaboration to deal with the opportunities to enhance and foster innovation.

Conclusion

This chapter develops a theoretical framework to help explain how being the BOP market can enhance innovation performance through collaboration. The innovation performance improvements in export firms have become a topic of interest to many academicians, practitioners, and researchers. We conclude that innovation performance improvement is dominant through social performance. We also figured out that patterns of innovation performance improvements are driven by an increased level of collaboration. There is a growing interest that BOP represents important market development opportunities. The findings have demonstrated the fact that social performance and innovation performance can co-exist given the focus on the inter-organizational collaboration. Therefore, converting less developed partners and enhancing the well-being and health and safety issues in the BOP markets requires a strong focus on collaboration with their focus on social and environmental issues. The study suggests that collaboration and social performance is the essential living approach for the manufacturing firms in South Asian countries, meaning that sustainability initiatives are essential for driving innovation performance.

We have also used the knowledge base view to frame arguments on how collaboration between buyers and suppliers can facilitate the manufacturing firms to enhance social performance and innovation performance in BOP markets. Most of the international buyer firms have generally focused on economic pyramids; they have not focused on the well-being of the individual, like health and safety issues and the inclusion of social equality in developing countries. Local firms often have little knowledge concerning the best practices required by their buyers or partners. As such, when international buyer firms enter the BOP markets, they may also leverage firms' existing resources to build local firms' knowledge resources and skills to develop new innovative process and products. For example, Adidas, the largest buyer of footballs within the Pakistan sports manufacturing industry, formed a partnership with the Forward Sports Group, a local firm operating in Sialkot. Adidas initially worked with the forwarding sports company to transfer the technology to serve the needs of the production facility and to develop a new process that is significantly different from their previous practices.

BOP markets are attractive to international buyers. To be socially sustainable, collaboration at the bottom must follow a double bottom collaboration (including social and environmental). The collaboration enables the local firm to implement social sustainability practices, such as providing an equal wage, no support of child labour, establishing equal rights for the workers (both female and male), establishing the sexual harassment system in place, and improving health and safety issues. This supports our arguments that enabling suppliers' firms to improve social performance through buyer collaborations may hold the key to innovation performance.

The primary contribution of this study is the offering of an empirical understanding of how inter-organizational collaboration on a double bottom line (social and environmental) can enable BOP markets' development and improvement in innovation performance. Consistent with the findings of the previous study (Schuster & Holtbrügge, 2014), the findings suggest that cross-border collaboration supports firms in adapting to a mutual understanding of mutual responsibilities in product and process to reduce the environmental impact. Although BOP literature has found that global firm collaboration is a strategy for market development and innovation, it has not yet recognised the role of inter-organizational collaboration in order to develop and improve social performance at the level of manufacturers' industry. The findings of this study demonstrate that the export-manufacturing firms need inter-organizational global collaborations for social sustainability of the firms located in the BOP to create innovations in products and process. In sum, our findings suggest that social performance improvement possesses a substantial influence on the ability of firms to maintain innovation performance improvement in an emerging country, such as Pakistan.

Managerial and practical applications

The following managerial implications may be derived from our research, especially for managers in manufacturing firms in Pakistan and other developing countries' economies with similar social sustainability challenges. Firstly, our results suggest that managers should follow collaboration strategies to identify what their firm needs, but only to a certain point if they are looking for better social performance in the BOP markets. Secondly, managers have to evaluate if the proposed beneficial effects of collaboration outweigh the negative consequences of social issues. However, this should be done with caution, as more dependency might not affect the firm's ability to survive independently. The present study gives empirical evidence for the fact that the development of health, safety, and labour standards can have a positive impact on innovation performance.

Thirdly, the findings suggest that the firms with a socially sustainable performance can differentiate their offering from those of competitors. In particular, this study helps the managers to understand that modes of innovation performance improvements require sustainability culture to be more deeply embedded in the routine firm operations (Adams, Jeanrenaud, Bessant, Denyer, & Overy, 2016). If innovation performance improvement is not visible, we suggest that managers should assess the overlapping of culture. The results of this study also suggest that the supplier should be aware of the partner cultural practices for development of relational activities accordingly.

Fourthly, our findings offer insights for practising managers. International partners (buyers) have to create a mechanism that shifts the BOP markets from a low to superior innovation performance. Creating such a mechanism should be seen as an investment, much like the development of training initiatives in plants and improve social performance. To develop more innovative solutions, two interventions are important providing collaboration and increasing the social well-being of the individuals: the access to the knowledge resources and skills that allows BOP markets in building new innovative solutions. It seems clear that access to knowledge resources and skills is a critical ingredient in improving the cycle of innovation performance.

The findings of this study have the capacity to offer a tool for learning about how well policies and programmes on sustainable development are delivering objectives. Policy makers should target different policies to a different group of industries, for example, to provide more resources to the small and medium enterprises (SMEs) in BOP markets as compared to the multinational corporations, which are mainly engaged in local business transactions (activities). These SMEs are an important player in the BOP market and their development can contribute to foster sustainability through innovation. Policy makers should develop industry-specific sustainability practices and should increase the efficiency of the labour force by providing training aiming at promoting a better understanding of the new sustainable development initiatives. Moreover, the mobility of retired senior employees from policy institutions to large companies may be beneficial to transfer their knowledge to firms seeking sustainable performance in all spheres of the triple bottom line.

Moreover, government support has focused on policy development and providing financial benefits. To develop more innovative solutions, two interventions are important – collaboration and increasing the social well-being of the individuals. The access of knowledge resources and skills allow BOP markets to build new innovative solutions. It seems clear that access to knowledge resources and skills is a critical ingredient in improving the cycle of innovation performance. Thus, the effectiveness of the implementation of human rights initiatives, health, and safety-related issues may also depend on the appropriate collaboration.

Future research studies

Despite the contribution, this study has limitations, which should be addressed in future research. There is always increasing popularity that BOP markets symbolise imperative expansion opportunities, irrespective of presenting substantial social sustainability improvement challenges. First of all, the sample used contains only Pakistani manufacturing firms. It would be interesting in the future to conduct a study involving other sectors to see whether the findings are also comparable to these firms. Second of all, future research studies should establish a link between innovation performance and economic performance by demonstrating which socially sustainable practices determine economic performance. Our measure of social performance was limited to a few items that may have failed to capture unique aspects of sustainability in manufacturing industries. Future research is needed to identify the unique elements of a social sustainability performance that can enhance social innovation. With respect to future research, the social innovation of foreign partners depends on external collaboration in BOP markets.

References

Adams, R., Jeanrenaud, S., Bessant, J., Denyer, D., & Overy, P. (2016). Sustainability-oriented innovation: a systematic review. *International Journal of Management Reviews, 18*(2), 180–205. https://doi.org/10.1111/ijmr.12068

Anisul Huq, F., Stevenson, M., & Zorzini, M. (2014). Social sustainability in developing country suppliers. *International Journal of Operations & Production Management, 34*(5), 610–638. https://doi.org/10.1108/IJOPM-10-2012-0467

Armstrong, J. S., & Overton, T. S. (1977). Estimating nonresponse bias in mail surveys. *Journal of Marketing Research, 14*(3), 396–402.

Arnold, D. G., & Valentin, A. (2013). Corporate social responsibility at the base of the pyramid. *Journal of Business Research, 66*(10), 1904–1914.

Awan, Usama. (2017). Mediation analysis of environmental training: perceived stakeholder pressure and environmental supply chain management practices. *International Journal of Research Studies in Management, 6*(1), 1–21.

Awan, Usama. (2019). Effects of buyer-supplier relationship on social performance improvement and innovation performance improvement. *International Journal of Applied Management Science, 11*(1), 21–35.

Awan, Usama, Khattak, A., & Kraslawski, A. (2019). Corporate social responsibility (CSR) priorities in the small and medium enterprises (SMEs) of the industrial sector of Sialkot, Pakistan. In *Corporate Social Responsibility in the Manufacturing and Services Sectors* (pp. 267–278). Berlin: Springer.

Awan, Usama, Kraslawski, A., & Huiskonen, J. (2018a). Buyer-supplier relationship on social sustainability: moderation analysis of cultural intelligence. *Cogent Business & Management, 5*(1), 1429346. https://doi.org/10.1080/23311975.2018.1429346

Awan, Usama, Kraslawski, A., & Huiskonen, J. (2018b). Governing interfirm relationships for social sustainability: the relationship between governance mechanisms, sustainable collaboration, and cultural intelligence. *Sustainability, 10*(12), 4473. https://doi.org/10.3390/su10124473

Awan, Usama, Kraslawski, A., & Huiskonen, J. (2018c). The impact of relational governance on performance improvement in export manufacturing firms. *Journal of Industrial Engineering and Management JIEM, 11*(3), 349–370. https://doi.org/10.3926/jiem.2558

Awan, U., Muneer, G., & Abbas, W. (2013). Organizational collaborative culture as a source of managing innovation. *World Applied Sciences Journal, 24*(5), 582–587. https://doi.org/10.5829/idosi.wasj.2013.24.05.1085

Awan, Usama, & Sroufe, R. (2020). Interorganizational collaboration for innovation improvement in manufacturing: the mediating role of social performance. *International Journal of Innovation Management*. https://doi.org/DOI: 10.1142/S1363919620500498

Awan, Usama, Sroufe, R., & Kraslawski, A. (2019). Creativity enables sustainable development: supplier engagement as a boundary condition for the positive effect on green innovation. *Journal of Cleaner Production, 226*, 172–185. https://doi.org/10.1016/j.jclepro.2019.03.308

Awaysheh, A., & Klassen, R. D. (2010). The impact of supply chain structure on the use of supplier socially responsible practices. *International Journal of Operations & Production Management, 30*(12), 1246–1268.

Bagozzi, R. P., & Yi, Y. (1988). On the evaluation of structural equation models. *Journal of the Academy of Marketing Science, 16*(1), 74–94.

Barney, J. B., Ketchen, D. J., & Wright, M. (2011). The future of resource-based theory revitalization or decline? *Journal of Management, 37*(5), 1299–1315.

Belz, F. M., & Krämer, A. (2008). Consumer integration in innovation processes. A new approach for creating and enhancing innovations for the base-of-the-pyramid (BoP)? In Kandachar P., & Halme M. (eds), *Sustainability Challenges and Solutions at the Base of the Pyramid: Business, Technolog.* London: Routledge.

Benner, M. J. (2009). Dynamic or static capabilities? Process management practices and response to technological change. *Journal of Product Innovation Management, 26*(5), 473–486.

Cao, M., & Zhang, Q. (2011). Supply chain collaboration: impact on collaborative advantage and firm performance. *Journal of Operations Management, 29*(3), 163–180.

Carey, S., Lawson, B., & Krause, D. R. (2011). Social capital configuration, legal bonds and performance in buyer–supplier relationships. *Journal of Operations Management, 29*(4), 277–288.

Carter, C. R., & Easton, P. L. (2012). Sustainable supply chain management: evolution and future directions. *International Journal of Physical Distribution & Logistics Management, 41*(1), 46–62. https://doi.org/10.1108/09600031111101420

Carter, C. R., & Jennings, M. M. (2002). Social responsibility and supply chain relationships. *Transportation Research Part E: Logistics and Transportation Review, 38*(1), 37–52.

Chen, L., Zhao, X., Tang, O., Price, L., Zhang, S., & Zhu, W. (2017). Supply chain collaboration for sustainability: a literature review and future research agenda. *International Journal of Production Economics, 194*(2017): 73–87. https://doi.org/10.1016/j.ijpe.2017.04.005

Chin, W. W. (1998). The partial least squares approach to structural equation modeling. *Modern Methods for Business Research, 295*(2), 295–336.

Cohen, J. (1992). A power primer. *Psychological Bulletin, 112*(1), 155–159

Dul, J., & Ceylan, C. (2011). Work environments for employee creativity. *Ergonomics, 54*(1), 12–20. https://doi.org/10.1080/00140139.2010.542833

Ehrgott, M., Reimann, F., Kaufmann, L., & Carter, C. R. (2011). Social sustainability in selecting emerging economy suppliers. *Journal of Business Ethics, 98*(1), 99–119.

Elkington, J. (1997). Cannibals with forks. *The Triple Bottom Line of 21st Century.* Canada: New Society Publishers.

Esfahbodi, A., Zhang, Y., Watson, G., & Zhang, T. (2017). Governance pressures and performance outcomes of sustainable supply chain management – an empirical analysis of UK manufacturing industry. *Journal of Cleaner Production, 155*, 66–78.

Fornell, C., & Larcker, D. F. (1981). Structural equation models with unobservable variables and measurement error: algebra and statistics. *Journal of Marketing Research, 18*(13), 382–388.

Gimenez, C., Sierra, V., & Rodon, J. (2012). Sustainable operations: their impact on the triple bottom line. *International Journal of Production Economics, 140*(1), 149–159. https://doi.org/10.1016/j.ijpe.2012.01.035

Gkypali, A., Filiou, D., & Tsekouras, K. (2017). R&D collaborations: is diversity enhancing innovation performance? *Technological Forecasting and Social Change, 118*, 143–152.

Gold, S., Hahn, R., & Seuring, S. (2013). Sustainable supply chain management in 'Base of the Pyramid' food projects – a path to triple bottom line approaches for multinationals? *International Business Review, 22*(5), 784–799.

Govindan, K., Seuring, S., Zhu, Q., & Azevedo, S. G. (2016). Accelerating the transition towards sustainability dynamics into supply chain relationship management and governance structures. *Journal of Cleaner Production, 112,* 1813–1823.

Grant, R. M. (1996). Toward a knowledge-based theory of the firm. *Strategic Management Journal, 17*(S2), 109–122.

Grekova, K., Calantone, R. J., Bremmers, H. J., Trienekens, J. H., & Omta, S. W. F. (2016). How environmental collaboration with suppliers and customers influences firm performance: evidence from Dutch food and beverage processors. *Journal of Cleaner Production, 112,* 1861–1871.

Haanaes, K., Arthur, D., Balagopal, B., Kong, M. T., Velken, I., & Hopkins, M. S. (2011). First look: the second annual sustainability & innovation survey. *MIT Sloan Management Review, 52*(2), 77–84.

Hair Jr, J. F., & Hult, G. T. M. (2016). *A primer on Partial Least Squares Structural Equation Modeling (PLS-SEM).* Sage Publications.

Halme, M., Kourula, A., Lindeman, S., Kallio, G., Lima-Toivanen, M., & Korsunova, A. (2016). Sustainability innovation at the base of the pyramid through multi-sited rapid ethnography. *Corporate Social Responsibility and Environmental Management, 23*(2), 113–128. https://doi.org/10.1002/csr.1385

Henseler, J., Dijkstra, T. K., Sarstedt, M., Ringle, C. M., Diamantopoulos, A., Straub, D. W., … Calantone, R. J. (2014). Common beliefs and reality about PLS: comments on Rönkkö and Evermann (2013). *Organizational Research Methods, 17*(2), 182–209.

Henseler, J., Hubona, G., & Ray, P. A. (2016). Using PLS path modeling in new technology research: updated guidelines. *Industrial Management & Data Systems, 116*(1), 2–20.

Henseler, J., Ringle, C. M., & Sarstedt, M. (2015). A new criterion for assessing discriminant validity in variance-based structural equation modeling. *Journal of the Academy of Marketing Science, 43*(1), 115–135.

Hull, C. E., & Rothenberg, S. (2008). Firm performance: the interactions of corporate social performance with innovation and industry differentiation. *Strategic Management Journal, 29*(7), 781–789.

Husted, B. W., & Sousa-Filho, J. M. de. (2017). The impact of sustainability governance, country stakeholder orientation, and country risk on environmental, social, and governance performance. *Journal of Cleaner Production, 155,* 93–102. https://doi.org/10.1016/j.jclepro.2016.10.025

Hutchins, M. J., & Sutherland, J. W. (2008). An exploration of measures of social sustainability and their application to supply chain decisions. *Journal of Cleaner Production, 16*(15), 1688–1698.

Khalid, R. U., Seuring, S., Beske, P., Land, A., Yawar, S. A., & Wagner, R. (2015). Putting sustainable supply chain management into base of the pyramid research. *Supply Chain Management, 20*(6), 681–696. https://doi.org/10.1108/SCM-06-2015-0214

Kistruck, G. M., & Beamish, P. W. (2010). The interplay of form, structure, and embeddedness in social intrapreneurship. *Entrepreneurship Theory and Practice, 34*(4), 735–761.

Kleindorfer, P., Singhal, K., & Van Wassenhove, L. (2005). Sustainable operations management. *Production and Operations Management, 14*(4), 482–492. https://doi.org/10.1111/j.1937-5956.2005.tb00235.x

Kolk, A., Rivera-Santos, M., & Rufín, C. (2014). Reviewing a decade of research on the base/bottom of the pyramid (BOP) concept. *Business & Society, 53*(3), 338–377. https://doi.org/10.1177/0007650312474928

Kotabe, M., Martin, X., & Domoto, H. (2003). Gaining from vertical partnerships: knowledge transfer, relationship duration, and supplier performance improvement in the US and Japanese automotive industries. *Strategic Management Journal, 24*(4), 293–316.

Lafferty, W. M., & Langhelle, O. (1999). Sustainable development as concept and norm. *Towards Sustainable Development* (pp. 1–29). London: Palgrave Macmillan.

Lakemond, N., Bengtsson, L., Laursen, K., & Tell, F. (2016). Match and manage: the use of knowledge matching and project management to integrate knowledge in collaborative inbound open innovation. *Industrial and Corporate Change, 25*(2), 333–352.

Large, R. O., & Thomsen, C. G. (2011). Drivers of green supply management performance: evidence from Germany. *Journal of Purchasing and Supply Management, 17*(3), 176–184.

Laursen, K., & Salter, A. J. (2014). The paradox of openness: appropriability, external search and collaboration. *Research Policy, 43*(5), 867–878.

Linton, J. D., Klassen, R., & Jayaraman, V. (2007). Sustainable supply chains: an introduction. *Journal of Operations Management, 25*(6), 1075–1082.

Liu, W., Zhu, R., & Yang, Y. (2010). I warn you because I like you: voice behavior, employee identifications, and transformational leadership. *The Leadership Quarterly, 21*(1), 189–202.

London, T., & Hart, S. L. (2010). *Next Generation Business Strategies for the Base of the Pyramid: New Approaches for Building Mutual Value.* Upper Saddle River, NJ: Pearson Education.

Lusch, R. F., & Vargo, S. L. (2014). *The Service-Dominant Logic of Marketing: Dialog, Debate, and Directions.* UK: Routledge.

Luzzini, D., Brandon-Jones, E., Brandon-Jones, A., & Spina, G. (2015). From sustainability commitment to performance: the role of intra-and inter-firm collaborative capabilities in the upstream supply chain. *International Journal of Production Economics, 165*, 51–63.

Macchion, L., Moretto, A., Caniato, F., Caridi, M., Danese, P., Spina, G., & Vinelli, A. (2017). Improving innovation performance through environmental practices in the fashion industry: the moderating effect of internationalisation and the influence of collaboration. *Production Planning and Control, 28*(3), 190–201. https://doi.org/10.1080/09537287.2016.1233361

Niesten, E., Jolink, A., de Sousa Jabbour, A. B. L., Chappin, M., & Lozano, R. (2017). Sustainable collaboration: the impact of governance and institutions on sustainable performance. *Journal of Cleaner Production, 155*, 1–6.

Nitzl, C., Roldan, J. L., & Cepeda, G. (2016). Mediation analysis in partial least squares path modeling. *Industrial Management & Data Systems, 116*(9), 1849–1864. https://doi.org/10.1108/IMDS-07-2015-0302

Nunes, B., Alamino, R. C., Shaw, D., & Bennett, D. (2016). Modelling sustainability performance to achieve absolute reductions in socio-ecological systems. *Journal of Cleaner Production, 132*, 32–44.

Nunnally, J. C., & Bernstein, I. H. (1994). The assessment of reliability. *Psychometric Theory, 3*(1), 248–292.

Pagell, M., & Wu, Z. (2009). Building a more complete theory of sustainable supply chain management using case studies of 10 exemplars. *Journal of Supply Chain Management, 45*(2), 37–56.

Palomares-Aguirre, I., Barnett, M., Layrisse, F., & Husted, B. W. (2018). Built to scale? How sustainable business models can better serve the base of the pyramid. *Journal of Cleaner Production, 172*, 4506–4513. https://doi.org/10.1016/j.jclepro.2017.11.084

Pavlou, P. A., & El Sawy, O. A. (2011). Understanding the elusive black box of dynamic capabilities. *Decision Sciences, 42*(1), 239–273.

Piening, E. P., & Salge, T. O. (2015). Understanding the antecedents, contingencies, and performance implications of process innovation: a dynamic capabilities perspective. *Journal of Product Innovation Management, 32*(1), 80–97.

Pisano, G. P., & Shih, W. C. (2012). Does America really need manufacturing. *Harvard Business Review, 90*(3), 94–102.

Podsakoff, P. M., & Organ, D. W. (1986). Self-reports in organizational research: problems and prospects. *Journal of Management, 12*(4), 531–544.

Podsakoff, P. M., MacKenzie, S. B., Lee, J.-Y., & Podsakoff, N. P. (2003). Common method biases in behavioral research: a critical review of the literature and recommended remedies. *Journal of Applied Psychology, 88*(5), 879–903.

Prahalad, C. K., & Hart, S. L. (2002). The fortune at the bottom of the pyramid. *Strategy & Business* (26).

Prahalad, C. K., & Hammond, A. (2002). Serving the world's poor, profitably. *Harvard Business Review, 80*(9), 48–59.

Prahalad, C. K., Di Benedetto, A., & Nakata, C. (2012). Bottom of the pyramid as a source of breakthrough innovations. *Journal of Product Innovation Management, 29*(1), 6–12. https://doi.org/10.1111/j.1540-5885.2011.00874.x

Ramani, S. V., & Mukherjee, V. (2014). Can breakthrough innovations serve the poor (BOP) and create reputational (CSR) value? Indian case studies. *Technovation, 34*(5–6), 295–305. https://doi.org/10.1016/j.technovation.2013.07.001

Reinartz, W., Haenlein, M., & Henseler, J. (2009). An empirical comparison of the efficacy of covariance-based and variance-based SEM. *International Journal of Research in Marketing, 26*(4), 332–344.

Rivera-Santos, M., & Rufín, C. (2010). Global village vs. small town: understanding networks at the Base of the Pyramid. *International Business Review, 19*(2), 126–139.

Sancha, C., Gimenez, C., & Sierra, V. (2016). Achieving a socially responsible supply chain through assessment and collaboration. *Journal of Cleaner Production, 112*, 1934–1947.

Sancha, C., Wong, C. W. Y., & Thomsen, C. G. (2016). Buyer–supplier relationships on environmental issues: a contingency perspective. *Journal of Cleaner Production, 112*, 1849–1860.

Sarkis, J., Helms, M. M., & Hervani, A. A. (2010). Reverse logistics and social sustainability. *Corporate Social Responsibility and Environmental Management, 17*(6), 337–354.

Schoenherr, T., & Swink, M. (2012). Revisiting the arcs of integration: cross-validations and extensions. *Journal of Operations Management, 30*(1), 99–115.

Schuster, T., & Holtbrügge, D. (2012). Market entry of multinational companies in markets at the bottom of the pyramid: a learning perspective. *International Business Review, 21*(5), 817–830.

Schuster, T., & Holtbrügge, D. (2014). Benefits of cross-sector partnerships in markets at the Base of the Pyramid. *Business Strategy and the Environment, 23*(3), 188–203.

Seuring, S., & Muller, M. (2008). From a literature review to a conceptual framework for sustainable supply chain management. *Journal of Cleaner Production, 16*(15), 1699–1710. https://doi.org/10.1016/j.jclepro.2008.04.020

Subrahmanyan, S., & Tomas Gomez-Arias, J. (2008). Integrated approach to understanding consumer behavior at bottom of pyramid. *Journal of Consumer Marketing, 25*(7), 402–412.

Tarafdar, M., Anekal, P., & Singh, R. (2012). Market development at the bottom of the pyramid: examining the role of information and communication technologies. *Information Technology for Development, 18*(4), 311–331. https://doi.org/10.1080/026 81102.2012.690172

Tavassoli, S. (2015). Innovation determinants over industry life cycle. *Technological Forecasting and Social Change, 91*, 18–32.

The Economic Times. (2018). Pakistan remains official football provider for FIFA World Cup. Retrieved from https://economictimes.indiatimes.com/news/sports/pakistan-remains-official-football-provider-for-fifa-world-cup/new-ball-for-knockout-phase/slideshow/64827738.cms

Tribune, T. E. (2014). Football: Sialkot workers fire 'Brazuca' ball to Brazil. Retrieved from https://tribune.com.pk/story/716857/football-pakistan-workers-fire-brazuca-ball-to-brazil/

Un, C. A., & Asakawa, K. (2015). Types of R&D collaborations and process innovation: the benefit of collaborating upstream in the knowledge chain. *Journal of Product Innovation Management, 32*(1), 138–153. https://doi.org/10.1111/jpim.12229

United Nations Statistical Commission. (2017). Global indicator framework for the Sustainable Development Goals and targets of the 2030 Agenda for Sustainable Development. UN Resolution A/RES/71/313. Retrieved from https://unstats. un. org/sdgs/indicators/Global Indicator Framework_A. RES. 71.313 Annex.pdf

Vachon, S., & Klassen, R. D. (2008). Environmental management and manufacturing performance: the role of collaboration in the supply chain. *International Journal of Production Economics, 111*(2), 299–315. https://doi.org/10.1016/j.ijpe.2006.11.030

WCED. (1987). Report of the World Commission on Environment and Development: Our CommonFuture. *Our Common Future, 17*, 1–91. Retrieved from https://idl-bnc-idrc.dspacedirect.org/bitstream/handle/10625/152/WCED_v17_doc149.pdf?sequence=1

Webb, J. W., Kistruck, G. M., Ireland, R. D., & Ketchen Jr, D. J. (2010). The entrepreneurship process in base of the pyramid markets: the case of multinational enterprise/nongovernment organization alliances. *Entrepreneurship Theory and Practice, 34*(3), 555–581.

Wood, D. J. (1991). Corporate social performance revisited. *Academy of Management Review, 16*(4), 691–718.

Yawar, S. A., & Seuring, S. (2017). Management of social issues in supply chains: a literature review exploring social issues, actions and performance outcomes. *Journal of Business Ethics, 141*(3), 621–643.

Appendix A

Scale items	
	Collaboration (Cronbach's alpha = 0.753)
	Please indicate the degree to which you agree to the following statements concerning your company's efforts to engage with your key customers (circle an answer for each item). 1: not at all, 2: a limited extent, 3: slightly improve, 4: neutral, 5: a moderate extent, 6: a great extent, 7: a very great extent
COL1	Making joint decisions about ways to reduce the environmental impact of our process.
COL2	Developing a mutual understanding of responsibilities regarding performance.
COL3	Working together to reduce the environmental impact of our activities.
COL4	Conducting joint planning to anticipate and resolve workers' health and safety-related problems.
	Social performance (Cronbach's alpha = 0.819)
	To what extent does each of the following statements you agreed or disagreed that your firm has improved performance. Please use the following scale to record an answer for each statement listed below (circle an answer for each item).1: not at all, 2: a limited extent, 3: slightly improve, 4: neutral, 5: a moderate extent, 6: a great extent, 7: a very great extent
SSP1	We have reduced the number of industrial accidents.
SSP2	We have improved child labour employment in our facilities.
SSP3	We have improved employee level of satisfaction with policies (social security systems, job security).
SSP4	We have improved safety and labour conditions in our facilities
	Innovation performance (Cronbach's alpha = 0.778)
	To what extent do you agree employee has contributed to improving you? Please use the following scale to record an answer for each statement listed below (circle an answer for each item). 1: strongly disagree, 2: disagree, 3: somewhat disagree, 4: neither agree nor disagree, 5: somewhat agree, 6. agree, 7: strongly agree
IPF1	Process design
IPF2	Product design
IPF3	Ability to conformances to specification
IPF4	Ability to develop new products

Part II

Drivers and barriers of BOP markets

3 Institutional voids and strategic responses by multinational corporations in Base of the Pyramid markets in Asia

Anne H. Koch

Introduction

For a long time, the Base of the Pyramid has been ignored by multinational corporations (MNCs). Many companies did not realise the potential for competitive advantage and growth in these markets for those who live in relative poverty across the world (Prahalad, 2010). However, this area of investigation is growing, with a number of scholars examining the initiatives of MNCs at the Base of the Pyramid (London & Hart, 2004; Tasavori, Ghauri, & Zaefarian, 2016; Tasavori, Zaefarian, & Ghauri, 2015). Scholars have suggested introducing social innovations – commercially viable innovations that address the pressing needs of low-income customers (Prahalad, 2004; Kolk, Rivera-Santos, & Rufín, 2014). However, contributions on Base of the Pyramid markets (BOP markets) have often been pursued without a consideration of the literature on institutional voids in underdeveloped markets. Institutional voids are defined as 'situations where institutional arrangements that support markets are absent, weak, or fail to accomplish the role expected of them' (Mair & Martí, 2009, p. 419). By neglecting this important focus, scholars fail to report the benefits of disrupting institutional voids, and how doing so can enable MNCs to compete in such markets and contribute to sustainable development.

Institutional distance is known to limit transferability from developed-country markets to BOP markets (Van den Waeyenberg & Hens, 2012). The problems that institutional voids create for firms have been well studied (McCarthy & Puffer, 2016; Doh, Rodrigues, Saka-Helmhout, & Makhija, 2017), but only recently has research focused on institutional voids as opportunities (Mair & Martí, 2009; Mair, Martí, & Ventresca, 2012; McCarthy & Puffer, 2016; Puffer, McCarthy, & Jaeger, 2016). Many studies focus on small or medium-sized enterprises in the context of institutional voids in emergent markets which inevitably have a large Base of the Pyramid. The following overview offers a critical reflection on how specific strategic responses can disrupt the weaknesses and absences of institutions and how MNCs can fulfil the role of change agents towards sustainable development in Asian markets.

This research advances understanding of institutional voids and strategic responses by MNCs in Base of the Pyramid markets. By using institutional theory and institutional forces (Scott, 2001) focus is placed on understanding the role that both formal and informal institutions play, or fail to play, in BOP markets in Asia. The regulatory dimension, including formal institutions, political risks, and strategic responses to voids, has been well studied. However, less elaborated are the cultural-cognitive and normative conditions that relate to informal institutions such as conventions or norms in this context (North, 1990). Examining the cultural-cognitive force of the applied framework reveals a new dimension of opportunities for sustainable development in BOP markets. Therefore, both the cognitive and normative dimension are important to develop a comprehensive typology of institutional voids and strategic responses for BOP markets.

This chapter will present existing empirical literature and theoretical insights that are the basis for a new approach to applying institutional theory to BOP markets. Strategic responses to specific institutional voids will be highlighted, allowing managers insight into creative ways to disrupt them. The discussion will allow scholars and managers to reflect on appropriate strategic responses and measures to take to enhance sustainable development.

The Base of the Pyramid and institutional voids and responses

Emerging markets in Asia not only include developing economies in Southeast Asia, but also transitional economies such as China, and parts of the former Soviet Union (Hoskisson, Lau, & Wright, 2000). They are in large part BOP markets with low purchasing power. Hence, they require innovations to be affordable at the bottom of the economic pyramid, reaching people with the lowest levels of income in any given society (Prahalad, 2006). Emerging markets with a large Base of the Pyramid compel a new approach to selecting and implementing strategies. Generally, new ventures in emerging markets have great difficulty fulfilling critical needs because in these economies, banks and various other strategic resources are severely underdeveloped (Li & Atuahene-Gima, 2002; Peng & Heath, 1996). However, recent research has suggested that institutional voids can also present opportunities for organizations in emerging markets (Mair et al., 2012; McCarthy & Puffer, 2016; Puffer et al., 2016).

In a seminal contribution Prahalad (2004) viewed the Base of the Pyramid as a source of innovation and growth opportunity to generate profits and set the stage for many scholarly contributions on BOP markets. The resulting BOP literature varies in terms of context, impact, and initiatives (Kolk et al., 2014). BOP literature on multinational corporations is of special interest to this chapter. In this literature authors often discuss and examine the need for large multinational companies to adapt business models to the private sector (Márquez, Reficco, & Berger, 2010; Mayer & Gereffi, 2010; Tasavori et al., 2015; Tasavori et al., 2016). For example, Tasavori et al. (2015) emphasise that

MNCs need to involve beneficiary stakeholders such as non-governmental organizations and BOP communities. Márquez et al. (2010) focus on business models, but also on internal structures and processes of socially inclusive business initiatives in Iberoamerica. BOP scholars have occasionally discussed environmental and social regulation and how barriers can be overcome with private governance (Mayer & Gereffi, 2010). Yet, what is less widely reported on is the cultural-cognitive weaknesses. Furthermore, institutional theory is not often referenced in discussions of Base of the Pyramid markets.

Prahalad originally envisioned that large MNCs had a central role to play in initiatives in BOP markets (Karnani, 2006b; Prahalad & Hammond, 2002). However, Kolk et al. (2014) who reviewed the literature over a period of ten years find that only a small number of reported BOP initiatives are actually led by MNCs. Similarly, Karnani (2006a) notes that almost all examples cited in Prahalad's (2004) book, are small not-for-profit organizations or local firms rather than MNCs. This chapter offers a contribution to the literature at the intersection of BOP markets and multinational corporations, specifically relating to strategic responses to informal institutional voids.

Some studies have used Scott's classification of institutional forces, regulatory, normative, and cognitive (Scott, 2001), to analyse the institutional environments of emerging markets. Such studies use surveys (Stephan, Uhlaner, & Stride, 2015) or case analysis as an approach (Barin Cruz, Delgado, Leca, & Gond, 2015; Mair & Martí, 2009; Mair et al., 2012; Puffer et al., 2010). The focus of these studies is usually not on MNCs, but on non-profit organizations. For instance, Mair and Martí (2009) examined financial voids and normative and cognitive elements based on a non-profit organization in Bangladesh. Mair et al. (2012) studied the same organization to focus on the market institutions of property rights and autonomy. Barin Cruz et al. (2015) analysed the implementation of a non-governmental banking cooperation in Haiti, and Puffer et al. (2010) used the concept of networking in Russia and China to explain how it helped overcome institutional weaknesses of regulations.

Previous research has also categorised response strategies for institutional voids. In a far-reaching review that included many non-market studies, Marquis and Raynard (2015) categorised institutional strategies in emerging markets along three dimensions: relational, infrastructure-building, and socio-cultural bridging, but they only occasionally applied them to institutional voids. Khanna and Palepu (2010) and Khanna, Palepu, and Sinha (2005) described a variety of other response strategies beyond filling voids which all clearly focused on the perspective of profit maximisation in emerging markets. Finally, the socio-cultural bridging strategies of Marquis and Raynard (2015) refer to local knowledge, but only marginally to labour-market institutions.

In summary, linking institutional voids and strategic responses to the institutional forces established by institutional theory can advance our understanding of actions of multinational corporations in BOP markets. The next section discusses the adaptation of the tri-facet framework to sustainable development of the challenging environments of these markets.

Adapting the tri-facet framework to sustainable development in BOP markets

The reflection of challenges and responses in BOP markets in Asia includes the regulatory, cultural-cognitive, and normative forces, as summarised in the tri-facet framework of Scott (2001). The analysis and discussion of institutional voids and strategic responses follows the distinction that regulatory institutions are formal institutions, while cognitive and normative forces are both informal institutions (Meyer & Peng, 2016). While economists tend to emphasise clearly defined and especially formal rules, organization theorists and even more so anthropologists (Peterson, 2016) focus on implicit normative and cognitive forces (Meyer & Peng, 2016). In most empirically observed institutional forms, we witness varying combinations of the regulatory, cultural-cognitive, or normative elements at work (Scott, 2001), for example, at state universities which work on knowledge and cognitions but also follow formal state rules (Koch, 2019). Government agencies are explicitly enforcing rules and laws in organizations, but cultural-cognitive and normative institutions such as cognitions, standards, and norms are also important to help sustainable development. The discussion below will categorize types of institutions and intermediaries by considering where the institutional forces primarily occur.

Strategic responses of management can fill voids and encourage sustainable development. The Sustainable Development Goals of the United Nations call all countries – poor, rich, and middle-income – to action in order to promote prosperity while protecting the planet. The sustainable development goals 'recognise that ending poverty must go hand-in-hand with strategies that build economic growth and address a range of social needs including education, health, social protection, and job opportunities, while tackling climate change and environmental protection' (United Nations, 2018). The following repeated aspects from this citation are included in the discussion on how MNCs can enter and/or compete in BOP markets and mitigate regulatory, socio-cultural, and normative weaknesses. The cultural-cognitive dimension includes 'education' and 'job opportunities', the normative dimension includes 'social protection', 'health', and 'tackling climate change and environmental protection'.

The direct citation of the United Nations illustrates another point which is central for a discussion on responses to institutional weaknesses. When considering 'strategies that build economic growth and address a range of social needs' (United Nations, 2018), the overarching goal for MNCs is to create conditions in underdeveloped markets that enable growth at the bottom of the pyramid. Enabling such growth means overcoming institutional weaknesses and working also at the higher end of the pyramid.

Further roadmap

The following sections categorise and apply strategic responses to institutional voids in BOP markets in Asia against the background of institutional forces (Scott, 2001). Identifying and synthesising weaknesses and matching strategic responses to the voids along these forces can help practitioners and scholars better understand when and how strategic responses can shape the institutional environment and intervene or disrupt business operations. Each section that follows offers several examples of strategic responses that MNCs have successfully implemented to fill institutional voids.

The institutional voids and responses presented here have been identified through an examination of the current literature. An initial search of academic databases was undertaken to identify academic literature and news reports on weaknesses or absences of institutions impacting underserved populations in Asia. At first, institutional voids and risk were used as search terms. Second, the three dimensions in the tri-facet framework of Scott (2001) and more specifically regulations, cognitions, culture, standards, and norms were used as search terms. The resulting literature was then reviewed and categorised to match the three dimensions of the tri-facet framework. In a next step, the search focused on exemplar responses by MNCs to institutional voids in Asian BOP markets. First, responses to institutional weaknesses were gathered and added to the discussion which sometimes, but not always, included company examples. The search then focused on identifying additional compelling company examples. Responses and example cases were selected that illustrate interesting and effective ways to respond to institutional weaknesses or absences in these markets. The selection excluded literature and case examples that did not focus on Asia and MNCs.

Institutional dimensions and strategic responses to institutional voids in emerging markets

The following sections review and discuss the selected barriers for business as they occur in Asian BOP markets. A discussion of the voids is followed by examples of appropriate strategic responses. Table 3.1 displays the associated types of institutions and intermediaries, the institutional voids, and matching strategic responses to fill such institutional voids.

Regulatory institutional voids and strategic responses

In most emerging markets the government plays a key role in supplying funds, information, and support services to firms to facilitate business dealings (Cui & Liu, 2000). Political turmoil and corruption can lead to unpredictable changes in government and industrial policy which can be adverse to any company (Sull, 2005), particularly those in emerging markets. Typical institutional voids in the regulatory domain are changing government leaders and administrators and changing government regulations.

Informal ties and relational governance can often compensate for the institutional voids left in the formal institutional infrastructure (Khanna & Palepu, 1997; Peng & Heath, 1996; Xin & Pearce, 1996; Luo & Chung, 2013).

Table 3.1 Application of the tri–facet framework to institutional voids and strategic responses in Asian BOP markets

Types of institutions and intermediaries	Institutional voids	Strategic responses	Examples of firms in Asia
Regulatory dimension			
Government agencies	• Void of changing government leaders and administrators	• Relational capital with government agencies and officials	Fraport
	• Void of government regulations	• Lobbying • Marketing approach • Business intelligence	Nike
Cultural-cognitive dimension			
Recruiting institutions	• Lack of access to qualified talent	• Third country hires • Self-initiated movers • Hiring local senior managers • Previous knowledge of firm members on advertisement channels	Adidas
	• Lack of employment recruiting services	• Internal redeployment of talents • Strategy of globalisation for recruitment and learning	Bertelsmann
Training institutions	• Lack of training and development for employees	• Quality training • Business group affiliation	Dasan Zhone Solutions
Normative dimension			
Labour market institutions	• Lack of unionisation and labour standards	• Market entry with MNE subsidiary • Monitoring by non-governmental Fair Labor Association • Monitoring market developments • Adaptation to market demands	Nestlé
Transportation institutions	• Poor public transportation system	• Product innovation	Mahindra
Banking institutions	• Poor banking service	• Service innovation	M-Pesa
Health care providers	• Lack of health care services	• Service innovation	Novartis

Empirical research suggests that managerial ties, not only with other firms but also government officials, are important in improving firms' performance (Peng & Luo, 2000). Connections with agencies, institutes, insiders, and influential decision makers can help reduce the effects of unexpected adverse policies (Sull, 2005). However, changes in political administrations can lead to special patronage, and, in some cases, extreme nepotism. Favouritism often results in the withdrawal of political support for foreign businesses. For instance, the difficulties faced by the German manufacturer Fraport in constructing a terminal in the Benigno Aquino Airport in the Philippines were fraught with conflicting preferences between the changing administrations. The contracts and agreements originally made by the sitting president were nullified by the incoming president. The change of government leader created significant difficulties for Fraport that spanned several years of litigious and contentious exchanges. The airport extension in the Philippines illustrates a strategy for economic growth in an emerging market with a large Base of the Pyramid.

Multinational corporations operating in BOP markets will likely experience voids in government regulations. When the athletic clothing giant Nike first entered China, it was surprised to find that its preference for the location of the production plant was contravened by the preference of local officials. Unable to persuade the officials, Nike started the plant in a second choice location. After years of relentless negotiations the company was granted permission to resume operations of the plant in a more favourable location, more in accord with its strategy and motivations. In this way, Nike was able to surmount the initial void of government support by forging closer relations with key players in the Chinese bureaucracy, using political savvy to overcome risk that arose from its initial poor location. The use of business intelligence methods and marketing helped to determine and enact this plan and enabled Nike to seize the opportunity when it presented itself.

Cultural-cognitive institutional voids and strategic responses

Strategic managers often need to work against cultural-cognitive institutional weaknesses and knowledge gaps in conducting business in emerging markets. Recruiting, educating, and training on how to navigate institutional voids can help MNCs deal with potentially weak or absent institutions. This includes shaping beliefs and motivating MNCs to disrupt institutional voids with social innovations and learning about cultural cognitions in a nation.

Institutional voids and strategic responses for recruiting

The lack of established local recruiting institutions in some emerging markets creates limited access to qualified talent (Khanna & Palepu, 2010). The impact of lacking service providers and lack of talent can severely affect companies' recruitment. Mobility constraints have led organizations to seek novel strategic responses in attempting to fill voids by drawing upon new sources of talent, such as self-initiated movers (Koch, 2019). Research suggests that 'Third Country Nationals' – individuals hired by a MNC to operate in a host country, but whose nationality is neither that of the host country nor the country-of-ownership of the MNC – may be growing in importance (Farndale, Scullion, & Sparrow, 2010). For example, the clothing manufacturer Adidas now routinely utilises an international external hiring approach. More than half of the recruits to its corporate headquarter who receive international mobility benefits are nationals from third countries. Adidas intends to further increase the number of international external hires by 20% (Farndale, Scullion, & Sparrow, 2010). The routine of sourcing talent through self-initiated movers and third country nationals is a promising strategic response for companies to close the talent gap.

When companies are seeking to compensate for lacking or weak recruiting intermediaries, firms can try to create competitive advantage by hiring local senior managers (Marquis & Raynard, 2015). Another option is to redeploy talents internally as alternative to external hiring. For instance, the German multimedia firm Bertelsmann offers a CEO programme that brings high-performing employees from emerging markets into their headquarters. Here, they gain exposure to the range of functional and geographical issues they can expect to encounter as leaders. Having spent a couple of years at the headquarters, recruits then compete for senior roles in local or regional markets offered by the company (Luo, 2016). The strategy of redeployment is especially useful and feasible in larger multinational firms. Due to their larger size, these firms can draw from more employees. They may also have more extensive internal training available to employees before redeploying them.

Institutional voids and strategic responses for employee training

Educational institutions and multinational corporations do not always have adequate knowledge about risk, voids, and strategic responses in emerging markets. To compensate, private management training can help address these knowledge gaps. For instance, Dasan Zhone Solutions, a provider of telecommunications networking equipment headquartered in California, operates in more than 20 countries worldwide. It lacks qualified personnel in Vietnam because IT universities in the country do not offer training on chip programming. Graduates are intelligent and possess sound knowledge, but do not have skills and practical experience and so work at a slow pace and are ineffective (*VN Economic Times*, 2018). It is not only hard to find domain experts in new technologies, but also foreign-language and soft skills are hurdles for Vietnamese in international R&D activities. However, the CEO of the company remains optimistic about Vietnam's human resources. He trusts that, with appropriate training, employees will gain the experience to catch up with international colleagues over time.

MNCs can also hire local managers or workers who have networks to help build interorganizational relationships with local business partners and government agencies (Luo, 2011). Further, many of the large business groups, for example in India, have internal management development programmes, often with dedicated facilities (Khanna & Palepu, 2010) that are typically geared towards developing the skills of experienced managers. Some groups have even instituted training programmes for all levels of employees to develop a broad range of human capital.

Normative dimension: institutional voids and strategic responses

Existing literature has explored how MNCs can lack supporting infrastructure in product markets (Khanna, Palepu, & Sinha, 2005; Marquis & Raynard, 2015). Reference is made to underdeveloped social, technological, and physical infrastructures, including basic physical and organizational structures and facilities, such as buildings, roads, and power supplies needed for the operation of a society or enterprise. Infrastructural weaknesses in emerging markets can also include challenges due to the lack of, or inefficiency of, assets within supply chains (King, 2001), transportation, energy supply, and information technologies. Such infrastructural deficiencies or absences can severely hinder firms' efficient operations, as well as limit socially engaged businesses in BOP markets. The normative institutional force is a less elaborated dimension with respect to informal institutions in emerging markets. Here specific attention is given to normative institutional weaknesses in emerging markets, and how MNCs can overcome them by setting labour and environmental standards and/or by engaging in social innovation.

Labour and environmental standards

A lack of unionisation in emerging markets can have adverse effects on labour standards, such as long working hours, difficulties for workers to obtain sick leave, and child labour. As a remedy, companies can circumvent low labour standards by market entry with an MNC subsidiary that employs higher labour standards (Caves, 1996). Companies can also receive help with monitoring labour standards and rights from the Fair Labor Association (FLA), a non-governmental organization that aims to protect workers in organizations worldwide (Valente & Crane, 2010). For example, since 2012, the world's largest food company, Nestlé, has agreed to have the FLA monitor them (Gretler, 2015).

Employees from local areas are generally paid a much lower wage than transferred employees, creating both expectations and possibly jealousy of higher salaries. If employees from developed countries are seen to enjoy a more affluent lifestyle than local employees, it can challenge the cooperation between both parties in an MNC. Ultimately, if corporations learn to set more flexible pay scales for executives this may be one way of allowing practices that retain the best managers (Hoskisson et al., 2000). Such a strategic response can counteract the weaker or absent regulatory force of unions which can reduce tensions caused by unequal payment.

Environmental protection programmes, funding by the government, and ecological standards can be severely lacking in emerging markets. The environment cannot sustain long-term resource harvesting and the impact of pollution. Without government support for sustainability, a firm seeking to expand into emerging markets needs to think about environmentally friendly solutions. The goal should be to employ strategic responses that follow environmental and social standards. For instance, the Global Reporting Initiative (GRI) promotes a standardised set of environmental, social, and governance metrics for corporations (Marquis & Raynard, 2015) to enable them to achieve the highest social and environmental standards.

Social innovations

The responses of the following three multinational corporations all demonstrate disruption of weak or absent infrastructures by social innovation in form of new products and services. By adapting the responses to social needs in Asian BOP markets, such as transportation, banking, and health care, MNCs can help manage voids and facilitate sustainable development.

Transportation needs

Public transportation systems are generally not as well established in BOP markets as in developed markets. However, their importance must not be overlooked since well-developed transportation infrastructures can help employees travel to work and allow businesses to reach their goals. The following form of transportation can also help tackle climate change and environmental protection. If introduced in a systematic manner, battery-run rickshaws have been shown to offer low-emitting complementary transport for low-income communities, who suffer most from a lack of transport facility (Ali, 2011). Mahindra Electric, the electric vehicle division of Mahindra Group, has introduced the Alfa Mini electric rickshaw into the Indian market followed by the new Treo electric three wheeler rickshaw. Electric rickshaws are a more viable alternative to the current autorickshaws which are widely distributed in Asian markets and very polluting. Two versions of Mahindra's Treo electric vehicles have been launched, a three seater and a five seater which will serve as options for last mile connectivity in larger cities. They use the latest lithium-ion battery technology. Compared to other similar batteries this battery technology is more durable, lasts longer, and presents a low maintenance option (Daniels, 2018). Though originating in Karnataka, a state in southwest India, the Treo rickshaw will be available in more cities and states over the coming years.

Banking needs

Another fundamental need in emerging markets is personal banking (Onsongo, 2017) and financing of entrepreneurship (Chakrabarty & Bass,

2013) for small entrepreneurs and multinational corporations. An example of a strategic response to this void is M-PESA, a mobile phone-based money transfer, financing, and microfinancing service developed in 2007 by Vodafone for Safaricom and Vodacom. For the Base of the Pyramid, the price of the service should be affordable to those of low socio-economic status. M-PESA's mobile app services are provided free of charge, and the company receives its profit from a commission deducted from users' accounts for every transaction (Linna, 2012). To create M-PESA's service innovation, existing technology was applied to a new context. Enabling a faster and safer transfer of money, the service innovation resulted in significant economic value to marginal sections of society (Ashwin, 2012). The service has become the largest mobile network operator in Kenya and Tanzania in Africa, with billions of subscribers in Asia, thus ensuring billions of people who have access to a mobile phone, but no bank account can send and receive money.

Health care needs

Often health care infrastructure is not as well established in BOP markets. Gaps in service include offering enough medical services and supplies to serve the entire population. India is one such country constrained by a limited health care service. Unfortunately, over 80 percent of the population cannot afford the cost of health care and insurance is unavailable to most (Prahalad, 2006). An example of a meaningful void-filling strategic response with a service innovation is Swiss drug maker Novartis. The Novartis Access initiative launched in 2015 in India and has since expanded into many other countries. The initiative produces 15 patented and off-patent medicines focused on cardiovascular disease, respiratory disease, breast cancer, and diabetes. The initiative makes the medicines available in 30 low- and low-middle-income countries. The medicines are provided at an average factory price of $1 per month per treatment (World Economic Forum, 2016). Novartis is not the only example of such an initiative for donated or price-reduced medicines. The biopharmaceutical industry has increased its commitment to improving access to medicines in low- and middle-income countries. Many global biopharmaceutical companies are increasingly establishing initiatives in low- and middle-income countries which provide access to medicines (Rockers, Wirtz, Umeh, Swamy, & Laing, 2017). Such initiatives that provide access to otherwise unavailable or expensive medicines help fill the void of health care needs and support sustainable development.

These examples illustrate the normative force of the applied tri-facet framework and span a wide range of industries. As demonstrated, companies do not have to attempt to set better labour standards to fill institutional voids in the normative domain. Instead they can aspire to think innovatively to develop new products and services driven by desires to enable growth and help underserved populations.

Implications and conclusions

Managerial implications

As discussed, void filling strategic responses can be applied to address many different institutional voids. Strategic managers can actively help decrease most risks they encounter while conducting business in BOP markets with responses which disrupt the influences of such voids. Figure 3.1 brings

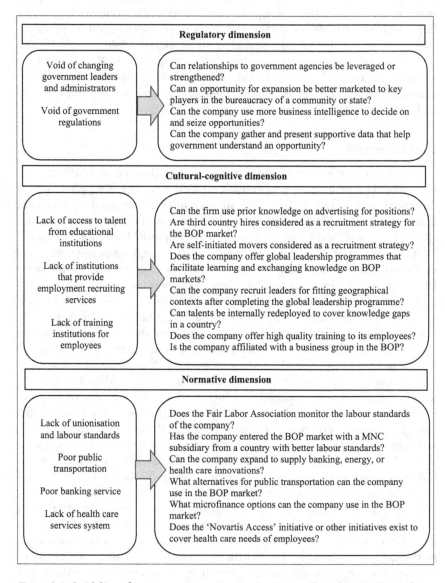

Figure 3.1 Guidelines for companies navigating institutional voids in BOP markets

together the lessons learned from the case examples and proposes guidelines for companies to navigate in BOP markets. MNCs can use the guidelines to reflect on the different institutional voids they face before identifying ways to address them.

By following the guidelines MNCs can benefit from the experience of other companies who have filled voids by adopting effective practices. Since institutional voids and risk perceptions differ by country, company, and even individual person, strategic responses will vary. To circumvent the biases and blind spots of a single decision maker, several key people within an organization should assess the type of risk for each institutional void.

Research contributions and conclusions

Extensive research over nearly two decades has focused on the challenges that institutional voids create for firms (McCarthy & Puffer, 2016; Doh et al., 2017). Only more recently has literature suggested that institutional voids can present opportunities for organizations in emerging markets (Mair et al., 2012; McCarthy & Puffer, 2016; Puffer et al., 2016; Onsongo, 2017). Naturally there is potential for sustainable development in these countries by improving and alleviating conditions of poverty in such markets with a large Base of the Pyramid. Our review adds to this research by identifying and evaluating institutional voids and strategic responses to those voids. The elaborations on strategic responses show that MNCs do not need to accept such limitations on business operations.

The literature has so far provided selected examples for strategic responses, but it lacks an assessment of selected strategic responses for individual voids that use the three institutional forces of the tri-facet framework. Specifically, the critical reflection of challenges and solutions extends previous literature by presenting exemplar strategic responses that MNCs can use to respond to regulatory, cultural-cognitive, and normative institutional weaknesses in Asian BOP markets.

The specific weak or absent institutional forces are key for understanding these voids and, as shown for all three areas, they provide opportunities for filling voids in BOP markets. Previous response typologies for voids conventionally focused on political systems and on intermediaries for capital, labour, and product markets (Khanna, Palepu, & Sinha, 2005; Khanna & Palepu, 2010). Without a primary focus on Scott's institutional forces, scholars partly neglected the role that institutions play and their role for failure or success of MNCs in bottom of the pyramid markets. In particular, they also neglected the role that informal institutions play for potential sustainable development in societies. The normative perspective of institutional voids offers many more possibilities for scholars to further explore and exploit opportunities for how firms can create disruptive change and increase social welfare simultaneously. Social entrepreneurs can enhance sustainable development by employing solutions in line with the United Nations agenda. Scholars could offer further contribution to the knowledge base on transitional economies by examining more social innovations that disrupt institutional weaknesses or absences.

Gathering more perspectives on cultural-cognitive institutional weaknesses and experiences of strategic responses in different contexts could lead to interesting insights on achieving economic development. Specifically, the routines for external hiring and redeployment may be a fruitful area of further inquiry with regards to how family business may achieve sustainable development of BOP markets. Scholars could build on the perspective presented here and further advance understanding of how informal institutions interact with, support, and counteract formal institutional arrangements. Finally, in-depth case studies on social ventures and innovations that strategically address so far underexplored institutional voids in the literature would also offer an interesting and important extension to understanding of BOP markets.

In conclusion, the exemplar strategic responses described in this chapter suggest ways to create disruption and shape institutional arrangements in Asian markets. The critical reflections and insights derived from applying the tri-facet framework to BOP markets will partly be transferable to studies and actions in other regions around the world that are in search of economic growth and sustainable development.

Acknowledgements

The author would like to thank Gerardo Ungson for his insights on the two company examples which are mentioned as part of the regulatory dimension of the framework. Further appreciation goes to Robert Barlow for his helpful comments on a previous draft of the manuscript.

References

Ali, T. (2011, May 30). Electric rickshaws run out of steam. Retrieved from https://www.thedailystar.net/news-detail-187825

Ashwin, A. S. (2012). Bridging institutional voids through new services: case studies and analysis. *Conference paper, Third International Conference on Services in Emerging Markets*, 1–13.

Barin Cruz, L., Delgado, N. A., Leca, B., & Gond, J.-P. (2015). Institutional resilience in extreme operating environments: the role of institutional work. *Business & Society, 55*(7), 970–1016.

Caves, R. E. (1996). *Multinational Enterprise and Economic Analysis.* Cambridge University Press.

Chakrabarty, S., & Bass, A. E. (2013). Encouraging entrepreneurship: microfinance, knowledge support, and the costs of operating in institutional voids. *Thunderbird International Business Review, 55*(5), 545–562.

Cui, G., & Liu, Q. (2000). Regional market segments of China: opportunities and barriers in a big emerging market. *Journal of Consumer Marketing, 17*(1), 55–72.

Daniels, P. (2018, November 15). Mahindra Treo 3, 4 seater electric rickshaw launch price Rs 1.36 L, 2.22 L – Including FAME subsidy. Retrieved from https://www.rushlane.com/mahindra-treo-3-4-seater-electric-rickshaw-launch-12287590.html

Doh, J., Rodrigues, S., Saka-Helmhout, A. U., & Makhija, M. (2017). International business responses to institutional voids. *Journal of International Business Studies, 48*(3), 293–307.

Farndale, E., Scullion, H., & Sparrow, P. (2010). The role of the corporate HR function in global talent management. *Journal of World Business, 45*(2), 161–168.

Gretler, C. (2015, September 1). Only ethically sourced cocoa for KitKat. Retrieved from www.bdlive.co.za/world/europe/2015/09/01/only-ethically-sourced-cocoa-for-kitkat

Hoskisson, R. E., Eden, L., Lau, C. M., & Wright, M. (2000). Strategy in emerging economies. *Academy of Management Journal, 43*(3), 249–267.

Karnani, A. G. (2006a). Mirage at the Bottom of the Pyramid. *William Davidson Institute Working Paper No. 835.* Retrieved from https://papers.ssrn.com/sol3/papers.cfm?abstract_id=924616

Karnani, A. (2006b). Misfortune at the Bottom of the Pyramid. *Greener Management International, 51,* 99–110.

Khanna, T., & Palepu, K. (1997). Why focused strategies may be wrong for emerging markets. *Harvard Business Review, 75*(4), 41–51.

Khanna, T., & Palepu, K. (2000). The future of business groups in emerging markets: long-run evidence from Chile. *Academy of Management Journal, 43*(3), 268–285.

Khanna, T., & Palepu, K. (2010). *Winning in Emerging Markets: A Roadmap for Strategy and Execution.* Boston, MA: Harvard Business School Press.

Khanna, T., Palepu, K. G., & Sinha, J. (2005). Strategies that fit emerging markets. *Harvard Business Review, 83*(6), 63–76.

King, J. L. (2001). *Operational Risk: Measuring and Modelling.* New York: John Wiley & Sons.

Koch, A. H. (2019). An international perspective on crafting strategic responses to institutional voids in emerging markets. *Working Paper.*

Kolk, A., Rivera-Santos, M., & Rufín, C. (2014). Reviewing a decade of research on the 'Base/Bottom of the pyramid' (BOP) concept. *Business & Society, 53*(3), 338–377.

Li, H., & Atuahene-Gima, K. (2002). The adoption of agency business activity, product innovation, and performance in Chinese technology ventures. *Strategic Management Journal, 23*(6), 469–490.

Linna, P. (2012). Base of the Pyramid as a Source of Innovation: Experiences of Companies in the Kenyan mobile sector. *International Journal of Technology Management & Sustainable Development, 11*(2), 113–137.

London, T., & Hart, S. L. (2004). Reinventing strategies for emerging markets: beyond the transnational model. *Journal of International Business Studies, 35*(5), 350–370.

Luo, X. R., & Chung, C. N. (2013). Filling or abusing the institutional void? Ownership and management control of public family businesses in an emerging market. *Organization Science, 24*(2), 591–613.

Luo, Y. (2011). Strategic responses to perceived corruption in an emerging market: lessons from MNEs investing in China. *Business & Society, 50*(2), 350–387.

Luo, Y. (2016). Toward a reverse adaptation view in cross-cultural management. *Cross Cultural & Strategic Management, 23*(1), 29–41.

Mair, J, & Martí, I. (2009). Entrepreneurship in and around Institutional voids: a case study from Bangladesh. *Journal of Business Venturing, 24*(5), 419–435.

Mair, J., Martí, I., & Ventresca, M. J. (2012). Building inclusive markets in rural Bangladesh: how intermediaries work institutional voids. *Academy of Management Journal, 55*(4), 819–850.

Márquez, P. C., Reficco, E., & Berger, G. (eds.) (2010). *Socially Inclusive Business: Engaging the Poor through Market Initiatives in Iberoamerica*. Cambridge, MA: Harvard University Press.

Marquis, C., & Raynard, M. (2015). Institutional strategies in emerging markets. *Academy or Management Annals, 9*(1), 291–335.

Mayer, F., & Gereffi, G. (2010). Regulation and economic globalization: prospects and limits of private governance. *Business and Politics, 12*(3), 1–25.

McCarthy, D. J., & Puffer, S. M. (2016). Institutional voids in an emerging economy: from problem to opportunity. *Journal of Leadership and Organizational Studies, 23*(2), 208–219.

Meyer, K. E., & Peng, M. W. (2016). Theoretical foundations of emerging economy business research. *Journal of International Business Studies, 47*(1), 3–22.

North, D. (1990). *Institutions, Institutional Change and Economic Performance*. Cambridge: Cambridge University Press.

Onsongo, E. (2017). Institutional entrepreneurship and social innovation at the Base of the Pyramid: the case of M-Pesa in Kenya. *Industry and Innovation, 26*(4), 1–22.

Peng, M. W., & Heath, P. S. (1996). The growth of the firm in planned economies in transition: institutions, organizations, and strategic choice. *Academy of Management Review, 21*(2), 492–528.

Peng, M. W., & Luo, Y. (2000). Managerial ties and firm performance in a transition economy: the nature of a micro-macro link. *Academy of Management Journal, 43*(3), 486–501.

Peterson, M. F. (2016). A culture theory commentary on Meyer and Peng's theoretical probe into Central and Eastern Europe. *Journal of International Business Studies, 47*(1), 33–43.

Prahalad, C. K. (2004). *The Fortune at the Bottom of the Pyramid: Eradicating Poverty through Profits* (1st edn). Upper Saddle River: Wharton School Publishing.

Prahalad, C. K. (2006). The innovation sandbox. *Strategy & Business, 44*, 1–10.

Prahalad, C. K. (2010). *The Fortune at the Bottom of the Pyramid: Eradicating Poverty through Profits* (4th edn). Upper Saddle River, New Jersey: Wharton School Publishing.

Prahalad, C. K., & Hammond, A. (2002). Serving the world's poor, profitably. *Harvard Business Review, 80*(9), 48–57.

Puffer, S. M., McCarthy, D. J., & Boisot, M. (2010). Entrepreneurship in Russia and China: the impact of formal institutional voids. *Entrepreneurship Theory and Practice, 34*(3), 441–467.

Puffer, S. M., McCarthy, D. J., & Jaeger, A. M. (2016). Institution building and institutional voids: can Poland's experience inform Russia and Brazil? *International Journal of Emerging Markets, 11*(1), 18–41.

Rockers, P. C., Wirtz, V. J., Umeh, C. A., Swamy, P. M., & Laing, R. O. (2017). industry-led access-to-medicines initiatives in low- and middle-income countries: strategies and evidence. *Health Affairs, 36*(4), 706–713.

Scott, W. R. (2001). *Institutions and Organizations: Ideas and Interests* (2nd edn). Thousand Oaks, CA: Sage Publications.

Stephan, U., Uhlaner, L., & Stride, C. (2015). Institutions and social entrepreneurship: the role of institutional voids, institutional support, and institutional configurations. *Journal of International Business* Studies, *46*(3), 308–331.

Sull, D. N. (2005, September 16). Emerging markets set the risk standard. *Financial Times,* London (UK).

Tasavori, M., Ghauri, P. N., & Zaefarian, R. (2016). Entering the Base of the Pyramid Market in India: a corporate social entrepreneurship perspective. *International Marketing Review, 33*(4), 555–579.

Tasavori, M., Zaefarian, R., & Ghauri, P. N. (2015). The creation view of opportunities at the Base of the Pyramid. *Entrepreneurship and Regional Development, 27*(1–2), 106–126.

United Nations (2018). *Sustainable Development Goals.* Retrieved from www.un.org/sustainabledevelopment/

Valente, M., & Crane, A. (2010). Private enterprise and public responsibility in developing countries. *California Management Review, 52*(3), 52–78.

Van den Waeyenberg, S., & Hens, L. (2012). Overcoming institutional distance: expansion to base-of-the-pyramid markets. *Journal of Business Research, 65*(2), 1692–1699.

VN Economic Times (2018, February 12). MNCs see benefits of R&D centers in Vietnam. Retrieved from https://english.vietnamnet.vn/fms/business/214175/mncs-see-benefits-of-r-d-centers-in-vietnam.html

World Economic Forum (2016). *Social Innovation: A Guide to Achieving Corporate and Societal Value,* Geneva/Switzerland: World Economic Forum, 1–34.

Xin, K. R., & Pearce, J. L. (1996). Guangxi: connections as substitutes for formal institutional support. *Academy of Management Journal, 39*(6), 1641–1658.

Part III

Roles, cooperation, and structure in BOP markets

4 Business–NGO collaborations in Turkey

The bottom-of-the-pyramid paradigm

Tuba Bozaykut-Bük

Introduction

Corporate sustainability management has been a critical concern in the current business environment in terms of meeting stakeholders' economic, social, ecological, and ethical expectations. All these expectations for a better business world paved the way for a 'sustainability revolution' (Starik & Kanashiro, 2013) representing a radical change in the ways and means of doing business. Within this context, corporate sustainability can be described as the mindset for enduring economic, social, and natural resources (Dyllick & Hockerts, 2002). Additionally, one of the most critical goals of corporate sustainability is to increase operational efficiency along with eco-efficiency due to decreasing costs stemming from the use of waste management strategies for effective resource consumption (Hockerts, 2015).

The inevitable rise of sustainability practices poses the question of how to coordinate business strategies with sustainability goals. Within this perspective, sustainability management emerges as a tool for achieving a competitive advantage related not only to an improved corporate reputation, but also to the *triple bottom line* (economic, environmental, and social) solutions that can find a place in the business strategies (Bonn & Fisher, 2011; Porter & Kramer, 2007). Thus, it is suggested that sustainability is an internal part of institutional strategies for long-term social and economic returns.

From a marketing-oriented perspective, it is also argued that sustainability should be used to create competitiveness by generating new market opportunities (Hockerts, 2015). In line with this approach, one of the most critical ways to create a new market is to offer products and services to the bottom-of-the-pyramid (BOP). To Prahalad (2006, 2012), companies can generate new markets by designing and selling products to four billion poor people who earn around $2 a day. In other words, companies are advised to consider the BOP as potential new markets for profit generation by meeting the needs of disadvantaged populations (Prahalad, 2012; Prahalad & Hammond, 2002; Prahalad & Hart, 2002).

Concordantly, BOP groups face barriers to education, employment problems, poor health conditions, and social exclusion. Fighting against these problems, both BOP and society expect businesses to develop solutions. As the complexity of issues in need of solution requires more than one organization's effort (Rivera-Santos, Rufin, & Kolk, 2012), businesses collaborate with other partners in their attempts to approach BOP. Moreover, according to BOP studies, NGOs (non-governmental organizations) have always been one of the critical partners of businesses for enduring growth in terms of entering into markets of the low-incomed populations. Therefore, the business-NGO partnership has become widespread as businesses and NGOs start building collaborations more often than ever for an enduring world (Arya & Salk, 2006; Bendell, 2000; Overdevest, 2004).

Within the framework of sustainability management, this chapter aims to analyse business-NGO collaborations influencing the conditions of BOP populations in a developing country context (i.e. Turkey). According to Turkish Statistical Institute (TSI) 2018 data, Turkey has a gross domestic product (GDP) of $9.632 per capita. Also, Turkey ranks 64 out of 189 countries in the 2018 *Human Development Indices and Indicators* report, prepared by the United Nations Development Programme. In terms of economic poverty measures of income and material deprivation, according to TSI 2015 data, the severe material deprivations rate was 30.3%. The percentage of people who could not afford one-week (annual) holiday away from home, a meal with meat, chicken, fish (or vegetarian equivalent) every second day, and unexpected expenses was 71.4%, 35.8%, and 32.6% respectively. This data indicates poverty as an issue that requires attention from the Turkish society. However, there are no current published BOP focused research on Turkish business activities that can help in meeting BOP needs. Thereby, the following research questions are developed to gain a deeper understanding of business-NGO collaborations concerning BOP in Turkey:

Research Question 1: What are the types of collaborations which businesses develop with NGOs for BOP in Turkey?

The features of Turkish companies can also affect business-NGO collaborations related to BOP. For instance, the limited number of studies shows that companies who have strategic alliances with multinationals, along with companies that engage in foreign investment, are the pioneer organizations for social responsibility activities in Turkey (Ararat, 2008; Ozdora-Aksak & Atakan-Duman, 2016). The previous international research also provides support that foreign investors act as facilitators of sustainability management practices because they want to retain the responsible company image built in their home country for their shareholders (Albornoz, Cole, Elliott, & Ercolani, 2009). Moreover, when compared to emerging country companies, foreign partners can have more experience and knowledge of sustainability guidelines (Qi, Zeng, Yin, & Lin, 2013), and thereby guide the taking of responsibility for economic, ecological, and social outcomes in the host country. Consequently, the companies with foreign partners may be more involved in NGO interactions for sustainability practices.

Besides interaction with multinational companies, corporate sustainability practices and reporting can show industrial variances. In other words, companies depend on their industries to address different shareholders and thus can have different sustainability practices (Li, Toppinen, Tuppura, Puumalainen, & Hujala, 2011). In particular, environmental issues – especially the harm done to the environment and a firm's closeness to the final consumer – are more carefully reported in some industries (Cormier, Magnan, & Van Velthoven, 2005). Besides, previous studies have shown that companies operating in environmentally sensitive industries such as oil and gas extraction or mining show higher degrees of sustainability reporting (Michelon, 2011). These companies can be more prone to developing relationships with NGOs and working on sustainability solutions for their operations. In addition to industrial variances, firm age can also be related to NGO engagement, as a longer firm history would mean more knowledge, activities, and engagements related to sustainability (Meng, Zeng, & Tam, 2013). To examine if foreign investment, company age, and industry make a difference in terms of Turkish companies' collaboration with NGOs, the following research question is developed.

Research Question 2: Do the types of collaborations show variances in terms of a) foreign investment, b) age, and c) industry?

To answer the research questions, the chapter is structured as follows: the chapter firstly presents a discussion of BOP in Turkey and a literary background on business–NGO collaborations related with BOP markets. Subsequently the research methodology and findings are outlined. Finally, the results of the research are summarised, and suggestions are made for future researches.

BOP and business–NGO collaborations

The definition of poverty shows variance not only from country to country but also from time to time (Yurdakul, Atik, & Dholakia, 2017). Therefore, it becomes a difficult task to define and measure poverty. Further, poverty can be evaluated both by economic and sociological dimensions. Within the economic perspective, to the Poverty and Equity Data Portal of World Bank (2018), Turkey has been evaluated as an upper-middle-income country with a population of 80.3 million out of which 9.3% forms the poor. To World Bank data, international poverty line is calculated as $1.90 a day (2011 purchasing power parity) corresponding to 0.2% of the population in Turkey. On the other hand, lower middle-income class rate is 1.8% and the upper middle-class poverty rate is 9.9%.

On the other hand, from the sociological standpoint, it is argued that there are non-monetary forms of deprivations, and hereby some counterarguments are directed at monetary indicators such as poverty line or purchasing power parity (Deeming & Gubhaju, 2014). Additionally, poverty, as a multidimensional construct (Atkinson, 2003), includes educational, social, sanitary, and environmental deprivations (Barry, 1998; Karadag & Saracoglu, 2015; Limanli, 2017). Based on both economic and sociological approaches, the current study identifies BOP in Turkey as populations in need of social and economic support because they lack minimum wage, basic education, and health services and are open to any kind of discrimination (Adaman & Keyder, 2006).

Also, to Prahalad (2012), a universal BOP solution would not fit all countries or all industries and companies seeking growth should acquire a deeper understanding of BOP dynamics in the given context. Accordingly, Prahalad's main proposition is a win-win scenario in which the BOP needs would be met in return for new markets. This perspective also encourages companies to go beyond short-term philanthropic aids (BOP 1.0) and engage more in solutions to the BOP needs (BOP 2.0) (Mohr, Sengupta, & Slater, 2012). Additionally, BOP projects may target achieving economic and non-economic results as creating a sustainable image for the company and creating social value for society (Byiers, Guadagno, & Karaki, 2015; Hammond, Kramer, Katz, Tran, & Walker, 2007).

In this win-win scenario, NGOs are identified as non-governmental, non-profit-making social actors (Martens, 2002) with the aim to provide social and economic support for BOP. Therefore, interactions between businesses and NGOs for BOP are critical as NGOs provide valuable knowledge about BOP needs and thereby inspire businesses for new ways of production or service delivery (Prahalad & Hammond, 2002). For instance, to access developing country markets, multinational corporations (MNCs) can collaborate with local NGOs to attain local resources or to acquire knowledge related to social, economic, and legal frameworks (Prahalad, 2006). These collaborations have some positive social and economic consequences such as creating employment and increasing shared value and productivity (Byiers et al., 2015). Moreover, shared value is extended through the offering of products and services to disadvantaged populations and through productivity resulting from global value chains (Porter & Kramer, 2011).

Within this framework, one of the most encouraged interaction types between businesses and NGOs is the development of social innovation, which refers to permanent development for BOP. To Prahalad (2006, 2012), businesses start collaborating more than ever with NGOs for BOP projects for resource utilisation, especially for newly designed products and services. Further, NGOs can play an active role in obtaining insight into the lifestyles and needs of BOP populations (Kong, Salzmann, Steger, & Ionescu-Somers, 2002; Monzer, Rebs, Khalid, & Brandenburg, 2018). This kind of cooperation can result in social innovation and market penetration for businesses (Desa & Koch, 2014). Especially in the given cases of MNCs, NGOs would help decrease the risks and overcome institutional barriers for entering BOP markets (Webb, Kistruck, Ireland, & Ketchen, 2010). Along with detecting daily habits of BOP populations, local NGOs become partners to companies for 'community participation, the supply of education and health care, and contacts with government' (Rivera-Santos et al., 2012, p. 8).

From a company-centred perspective, studies approach BOP either as consumers of products or as producers and suppliers of the company (Kolk, Rivera-Santos, & Rufín, 2014). Therefore, the role of NGOs can be that of 'an active assistance approach' through which BOP as producers are supported in developing themselves for sustainability practices (Perez-Aleman & Sandilands, 2008). This approach would benefit all parties, as MNCs would ensure the quality related to BOP producers. Thereby BOP as producers would not be alone in their production processes and can have the chance of achieving a competitive advantage in the market.

NGOs also play a role in identifying and developing 'the dos and don'ts in the sustainability arena' (Christensen, Morsing, & Thyssen, 2017, p. 241). As the sustainability movement redefines traditional ways of doing business, companies start showing a tendency to maintain and express responsible business practices. Additionally, to show their sustainability-focused business mentality, they adopt worldwide standards of ethics or production processes and acquire certifications. NGOs are active in the formation of codes of conducts and certifications that pave the way to responsible business practices (Perez-Aleman & Sandilands, 2008). Therefore, adoption of standards and certifications can be explained as an answer to NGO and public pressure for sustainable practices. Accreditation also functions as a tool promoting legitimacy and facilitates the increase of companies' interactions with NGOs. In addition, with a proactive manner, companies can cooperate with NGOs to urge their suppliers to adopt codes of conduct for business processes (Gereffi, Garcia-Johnson, & Sasser, 2001; Gold, Hahn, & Seuring, 2013; Perez-Aleman & Sandilands, 2008).

Furthermore, ensuring sustainability standards and certificates find voices in BOP as improved working conditions with better incomes, less pollution, and better infrastructure (Gereffi et al., 2001). BOP populations mostly live in the suburban areas that can have infrastructure problems and pollution of all kinds. As social and business infrastructures become more qualified through these codes of conduct, the quality of both social and working lives of BOP populations would improve. For example, participating in a carbon disclosure project or acquiring ISO 140001 would help to reduce air pollution whereas labour codes of conduct can be regarded as a means of preventing wages that are lower than the minimum wage, gender-biased promotions and wages, the mistreatment of children or minorities, or attempts to prevent employees from participating in labour unions (Gereffi et al., 2001). Additionally, certifications such as ISO represent a standard for global responsible business practices and 'structured management standards' designed by a third party in the formula of sustainability (Malmborg & Mark-Herbert, 2010, p. 67). It is also argued that third-party certifications function as legal frameworks, especially for countries that do not have a legal context for protecting environmental resources (Malmborg & Mark-Herbert, 2010). For multinationals, these efforts create a standardised way of doing sustainable business regardless of the country in which they operate. Thus, all kinds of interactions, including participating in sustainability programmes, adopting sustainability standards, and ensuring certificates, emerge as critical collaboration topics for businesses and NGOs.

Another method of improving the life quality of BOP populations is to support NGOs that specialise in improving the conditions of disadvantaged groups. This support can be in terms of being a member, giving donations, becoming a sponsor, designing common projects, or taking consultation for employee volunteerism (Kourula, 2006; Kourula & Halme, 2008; Prahalad, 2012). Examples of the given kind of cooperation include being a member of an NGO that seeks to educate BOP populations in terms of childcare and supporting this NGO financially by providing scholarships. Another example is designing common projects with NGOs for qualified production techniques or input materials for BOP as suppliers. Additionally, when seeking to support BOP populations with disabilities through employee volunteerism or by providing philanthropic and financial support, companies can collaborate with expert NGOs, which specialise in understanding disabled people's needs.

Research methodology

To answer the research questions of the study, the sustainability reports of companies listed in the BIST Sustainability Index are analysed using qualitative content analysis to categorise business–NGO collaborations for BOP in Turkey. Sustainability reporting – an analysis tool for investigating sustainability issues – can be described as a voluntary exhibition of a company's economic, ethical, ecological, and social performance to stakeholders (Kolk, 2008). Therefore, companies listed in the Sustainability Index are selected, as these companies are evaluated based on their attitude towards issues like global warming, natural resources, health, and employment. Additionally, the indexed companies are publicly known for their sustainability performances in Turkey.

Forty-four companies are listed in the Sustainability Index for the time period between November 2017 and October 2018. These companies are chosen for analysis. The descriptive data (revenue, age, and foreign investment) of the companies presented in Table 4.1 is collected from the 'About Us' and 'History' and 'Financial Statements' sections of the corporate websites.

Companies listed in Table 4.1 have an average revenue of EUR 3,661,674,879. Among the companies, Polisan Group and Tav Group are the youngest (18 years) and İş Bank is the oldest (94 years); the average company age is 51. There is also a diversity in the industries: manufacturing (18), banking (7), holding (7), electricity (3), technology (3), wholesale and retail (2), transportation, (2) and communication (2). Only 15 out of 44 companies have foreign partners. Furthermore, it is found that some of the companies (Brisa, Doğan Group, Kordsa Global, Netaş, Pegasus, Petkim, TAT, Türk Telekom, Tüpraş, Tekfen Group, Türk Traktor, Vestel Enerji & Vestel White Appliances, and Zorlu Enerji) do not issue any sustainability reports while others (Çimsa, Garanti Bank, Koç Group, TAV, and TSK Bank) do not have a current or separate sustainability report for the given time period. Therefore, 25 out of 44 companies are found to provide a sustainability report that can be analysed to answer the research questions.

Table 4.1 Companies in BIST Sustainability Index (Nov. 2017–Oct. 2018)

	Company*	Net revenue (EUR)**	Industry	Age	Foreign investment	2017 Sustainability report available
1	Akenerji	450,266,464	Electricity	29	ČEZ (37%)	Yes
2	Akbank	3,398,786,408	Banking	70	-	Yes
3	Aksa Enerji	873,619,385	Electricity	21	-	Yes
4	Anadolu Efes	3,142,455,825	Manufacturing	49	1. AB InBev Harmony Ltd. (24%) 2. Oppenheimer Developing Markets Fund (6%)	Yes
5	Arçelik	5,058,401,214	Manufacturing	63	-	Yes
6	Aselsan	1,301,038,592	Technology	43	-	Yes
7	Brisa	556,829,120	Manufacturing	44	Bridgestone Corp. (43,6%)	-
8	Çimsa	361,791,232	Manufacturing	46	-	-
9	Coca Cola Turkey	2,068,228,155	Manufacturing	54	The Coca-Cola Export C. (20%)	Yes
10	Doğan Holding	2,543,290	Holding	59	-	-
11	Doğuş Automotive	3,208,825,485	Wholesale and retail	24	-	Yes
12	Eregli Iron-Steel	4,525,221,845	Manufacturing	58	-	Yes
13	Ford Otosan	6,150,798,544	Manufacturing	59	Ford Motor C. (41%)	Yes
14	Garanti Bank	1,070,267,233	Banking	72	BBVA (49.8%)	-
15	İş Bank	9,918,233,252	Banking	94	-	Yes
16	Koç Holding	23,996,844,660	Holding	92	-	-
17	Kordsa Global	603,195,540	Manufacturing	45	-	-
18	Logo Software	603,195,540	Technology	34	-	Yes
19	Migros Trade	3,724,283,252	Wholesale and retail	64	1. Moonlight (7%) 2. Kenan Invest. (14.8%)	Yes
20	Netaş Telecom	272,394,583	Technology	51	ZTE Cooperative U.A. (48%)	-
21	Otokar	433,318,447	Manufacturing	55	-	Yes
22	Pegasus	1,298,197,429	Transportation	28	-	-
23	Petkim	1,787,336,039	Manufacturing	53	-	-
24	Polisan Holding	181,947,017	Holding	18	-	Yes
25	Sabancı Holding	3,359,187,136	Holding	51	-	Yes
26	Sişecam Holding	2,747,207,524	Holding	83	-	Yes
27	Soda Sanayii	594,973,786	Manufacturing	49	-	Yes
28	T. Halk Bank	878,745,146	Banking	85	-	Yes
29	T.S.K.Bank	446,764,806	Banking	68	-	-
30	Tat	260,688,036	Manufacturing	51	1. Kagome Co Ltd. (3.7%) 2. Sumitomo Corp. (1.5%)	-
31	Tav Airports	505,833,299	Holding	18	Paris Airport (46%)	-
32	Tekfen Holding	1,817,265,291	Holding	62	-	-
33	Tofaş Turk Otomotive	4,239,758,738	Manufacturing	50	Fiat Chrysler Automobiles (37%)	Yes
34	Tüpraş	13,094,201,456	Manufacturing	35	-	-

(Continued)

Table 4.1 (Continued)

	Company*	Net revenue (EUR)**	Industry	Age	Foreign investment	2017 Sustainability report available
35	Turkish Airlines	9,655,097,087	Transportation	85	-	Yes
36	Turk Telecom.	13,094,201,456	Communication	23	Oger Telecom. (55%)	-
37	Türk Traktör	1,023,071,870	Manufacturing	64	CNH Industrial (37.5%)	-
38	Turkcell Com.	4,132,621,602	Communication	24	-	Yes
39	Ülker Biscuits	1,167,726,341	Manufacturing	74	Pladis Foods Limited (51%)	Yes
40	Vakıflar Bank	5,527,854,126	Banking	64	-	Yes
41	Vestel	2,937,120,874	Manufacturing	34	-	-
42	Vestel White Appliances	936,407,767	Manufacturing	21	-	-
43	Yapı & Kredi Bank.	6,383,740,534	Banking	74	Koc Financial Services (81,9%-out of 50% belongs to UniCredit)	Yes
44	Zorlu Enerji	939,609,223	Electricity	25	-	-

*Companies are listed in alphabetical order.
** Revenues converted to EUR at 2017 average EUR/TRY rate (=4.12).

When companies with a sustainability report are analysed, the same variance is seen in terms of foreign partnership, age, and industry. Only eight companies with a sustainability report have foreign partners and the average company age is 55. Also, nine companies operate in manufacturing, five in banking, three in holding, and two in electricity, technology, wholesale, and retail respectively. Finally, one company operates in transportation and one is in the communication industry. Therefore, no difference is found between companies with and without sustainability reports in terms of foreign partnership, age, and industry.

To categorise business–NGO collaborations, the researcher uses qualitative content analysis to analyse 25 sustainability reports. Content analysis is selected to make valid inferences from the reports and to identify business–NGO collaboration categories, as it is mainly described as 'a research technique for making replicable and valid inferences from data to their context' (Krippendorff, 1989, p. 403). For the coding process, sustainability reports for the year 2017 are downloaded from company websites. The coding process starts with already discussed collaboration categories in the literature as developing social innovation, acquiring certificates, being a member, being a partner, becoming a sponsor, giving donations, designing common projects, and taking consultation for employee volunteerism (based mainly on Byiers et al., 2015; Gereffi et al., 2001; Malmborg & Mark-Herbert, 2010; Mulgan, Ali, Halkett, & Sanders, 2007; Kong et al., 2002; Kourula, 2006; Kourula & Halme, 2008; Prahalad & Hammond, 2002; Prahalad, 2012; Perez-Aleman & Sandilands, 2008). Consequently, a deductive approach is adopted to create a coding system for analysis.

A sentence-based coding instrument and coding rules are developed (Milne & Adler, 1999) for understanding the categories of business–NGO collaborations related to BOP. Thereby, questions are developed as coding rules and each question is designed to categorise the business–NGO collaboration and determine whether the collaboration has any influence on the social, economic, or working environment of BOP. The coding rules are questions such as: 'Does the company provide financial support to an NGO?' (*giving donations*), 'Does the company form a partnership with an NGO?' (*being a partner*), 'Does an NGO certify the company's activities/services, etc.?' (*acquiring certificates*), and 'Does the collaboration affect economic/social/ working conditions of BOP?' (see Table 4.2). Then, by reading and rereading the first three companies, a detailed coding scheme is generated.

In the code generation process, the researcher recognises the subcategories that emerged for partnerships and memberships. The subcategories are also coded deductively based on Ashman's (2001) study on business–civil society collaborations. Ashman categorises these collaborations as strategic (covering core activities of both parties) and philanthropic (developed for social and ecological objectives). In addition to strategic and philanthropic collaborations, some studies indicate that businesses increasingly interact with NGOs that specialise in generating sustainability standards, codes, and guidelines for responsible business processes and environmental management (Perez-Aleman & Sandilands, 2008; Unerman & O'Dwyer, 2010). Also, sustainability-focused NGOs create an opportunity to form normative pressures and to exchange and transfer knowledge; they also help improve the sustainability management of businesses (Hartman, Hofman, & Stafford, 1999). Therefore, collaborations with sustainability NGOs seek to improve environmental management practices and adopt global sustainability standards. Consequently, the subcategories for the study are defined as *strategic/philanthropic/sustainability* based on an NGO's field of expertise and its closeness to the company's core business.

After the researcher codes all the data, the coding schema is discussed with an academic working on sustainability management for peer debriefing to see if there is a disagreement or discrepancy between the two researchers (Cutcliffe & McKenna, 1999). Through peer debriefing, face validity is used to evaluate the trustworthiness of the study (Hickey & Kipping, 1996; Elo et al., 2014). After reaching a mutual consensus in terms of the collaboration categories, the researcher once again checks the coding schema for stability (Krippendorff, 1980) and then finalises the coding schema. After all sustainability reports are read through and coded, each category is clearly defined and named (see Table 4.2). The names of the category are also discussed with the peer academic for consensus before being finalised.

Secondly, the defined categories are counted to find the frequency of business–NGO collaboration types that take place in 2017. The main aim is to track the number of collaborations and to find the profundity of companies' engagement with NGOs for BOP needs. Social innovation, for instance, is directly concerned with offering solutions to BOP problems and has the potential to create lasting positive solutions and long-term value compared to NGO membership. Thereby, the act of counting the collaborations aims to reveal the most or the least collaborated forms in terms of BOP in Turkey.

Thirdly, business–NGO collaborations are analysed in terms of age and foreign investment. As the average company age is 55, the companies are categorised accordingly into two groups. The first group consists of companies that are 55 years and over (13 companies) while the other group comprises companies that are younger than 55 years (12 companies). Additionally, companies are placed into two other groups: companies with foreign investment ($n=8$) and local companies ($n=17$). Then, independent t-tests are conducted to determine whether there is a difference in terms of business–NGO collaborations between companies that have longer histories and with foreign partners compared to younger and local companies, respectively. Also, the collaborations are to be analysed in terms of industrial differences. However, as the industry of the companies shows a great variance, business–NGO collaborations are not examined in terms of industry.

Research findings

The previous literature showed evidence that business–NGO collaborations comprise various forms to enhance the social and economic order of BOP. Within the scope of the literature, the detailed reading and coding process reveals five major collaboration forms that develop between companies and NGOs that have a potential influence on BOP: 1. *partnership*, 2. *membership*, 3. *sponsorship and donation*, 4. *standards and certificates*, and 5. *social innovation*. The definitions and the examples based on the category definitions are presented in Table 4.2.

Another contribution of the coding process is the recognition of subforms such as *strategic, sustainability,* and *philanthropic* in terms of partnership and membership categories. The core competence of NGOs and the main business function of the companies are the critical dimensions for determining these subcategories. For instance, Vakıfbank's partnership with Turkish Agricultural Credit Cooperatives for better credit solutions for farmers is given as an example of *strategic* because both Vakıfbank's and Turkish Agricultural Credit Cooperative's main function is to finance farmers and cooperatives in Turkey. Similarly, Ülker Biscuits uses cocoa as the main ingredient for products and Ülker has a *strategic* partnership with Processor Alliance for Cocoa Traceability and Sustainability (PACTS) to provide solar energy and clean water for cocoa producers in the République de Côte d'Ivoire. Ülker Biscuits is also a member of the World Cocoa Foundation to support sustainable solutions for cocoa production. On the other hand, Şişecam group, mainly a glass producer, conducts an ecological *sustainability* project named Glass Re-Class Again with the Environment Protection and Recycling of Packing Wastes Foundation to increase the awareness of recycling glass. Similarly, Anadolu Efes' membership in the Sustainable Development Association is an example of *sustainability* membership, as the Sustainable Development Association seeks to form a systematic dialogue about global and local developments in sustainability among its members. An example of a *philanthropic* partnership

Table 4.2 Business-NGO collaboration categories related to BOP

Coding categories	Definitions	Coding rules	Examples from the analysed sustainability reports
Partnership	a *Strategic partnership* comprises collaborations with NGOs that are closely connected to the company's core business operations. b *Sustainability partnership* refers to collaborations with NGOs that are working mainly for environmental management and sustainable development. c *Philanthropic partnership* covers collaborations with NGOs that are working mainly for social issues that have no connection to the company's core business.	1 Does the company form a partnership with an NGO? 2 Are the partner NGO's core activities related to the core company activities? 3 Are the partner NGO's core activities related to environmental management and/or sustainable development? 4 Are the partner NGO's core activities related to social development? 5 Does the collaboration affect economic/social/working conditions of BOP?	a *Strategic partnership:* Vakıfbank, a public bank for developing agriculture and cooperatives, develops a partnership with Central Union of Turkish Agricultural Credit Cooperatives for understanding farmers' financial needs b *Sustainability partnership:* Şişecam Group is a partner of the Environment Protection Foundation for the awareness of waste management c *Philanthropic partnership:* Yapı Kredi Bank partners with the Turkish Education Volunteers Foundation for children who can't access basic education.
Standards and certificates	Standards and certificates refer to interactions with NGOs that ensure responsible business practices and provide certificates for these practices.	1 Does an NGO certify the company's activities/services, etc.? 2 Is the company a signatory of a sustainability initiative? 3 Does the company participate to a sustainability programme designed by an NGO for acquiring sustainability standards? 4 Does the collaboration affect economic/social/working conditions of BOP?	• Akenerji received a leadership award for 2017 Turkey Water Reporting by Carbon Disclosure Program (CDP). • Akenerji prepared its sustainability report by following the Global Reporting Initiative's guidelines. • Akenerji has had ISO 9001 Quality, ISO 14001 Environment and OHSAS 18001 OHS since 2010.
Sponsorship and donation	Sponsorship and donation refer to financial, material, or service support to NGOs.	1 Does the company provide financial support to an NGO? 2 Does the company sponsor an NGO activity? 3 Does the collaboration affect economic/social/working conditions of BOP?	• Polisan Group sponsored the Istanbul Carbon Summit held by the Sustainable Production and Consumption Association. • Eregli Iron Steel provided financial support to the Black Sea Eregli Association for the Disabled. • Ford Otosan financially supported the Turkish Red Crescent.

(Continued)

Table 4.2 (Continued)

Coding categories	Definitions	Coding rules	Examples from the analysed sustainability reports
Membership	Membership refers to a systematic dialogue between the company and NGO. Like partnership, membership can be *a. strategic, b. sustainable, and c. philanthropic* based on the NGO's field of expertise and its closeness to the company's core business.	1 Is the company a member of an NGO? 2 Does the membered NGO specialise in the company's core activities? 3 Does the membered NGO specialise in sustainability issues? 4 Does the membered NGO specialise in social development? 5 Does the collaboration affect economic/social/ working conditions of BOP?	*Strategic membership:* • Ülker Biscuits is a member of the World Cocoa Foundation to support cocoa production. *Sustainability membership:* • Anadolu Efes is a member of the Sustainable Development Association. *Philanthropic membership:* • Otokar, an automotive firm is a member of Turkish Volunteers for Education.
Social innovation	Social innovation comprises collaborations with NGOs to generate new ideas to both offer new products/ services and meet the social and economic needs of BOP.	1 Do the company and NGO collaborate for developing new products/services? 2 Do the newly developed products/services answer BOP's needs? 3 Does the collaboration affect economic/social/ working conditions of BOP?	• Turkcell has developed 'Hello Hope Project' with Turkish Red Crescent to design a software program that would meet the social needs of refugees in Turkey • Ford Otosan has developed 'Hope Café Project' with the Hope to Kids with Cancer Foundation; the project creates employment opportunities for the family of kids with cancer by offering them pick-up cars • Coca Cola Turkey has developed 'My Dear Teach Project' with Anadolu Group Foundation to offer opportunities for youth to develop sustainable solution for their communities.

would be Yapı Kredi Bank's partnership with the Education Volunteers Foundation for children lacking basic education. In this project, Yapı Kredi Bank and Turkish Education Volunteers Foundation provide non-elementary school children contemporary education opportunities such as developing reading skills, creative thinking habits, and discussion skills.

Secondly, business-NGO collaborations that influence BOP are counted to find the total number and the intensity of the interactions that take place in 2017. The total number of business-NGO collaborations in 2017 is 207, of which 85 interactions relate to *standards and certificates*. Only nine collaborations are targeted at creating *social innovation* (see Table 4.3). Additionally,

Table 4.3 The number of business–NGO collaborations related to BOP in 2017

Company	Standards and certificates	Partnership			Membership			Sponsorship and donation	Social innovation
		Strategic	Sustainability	Philanthropic	Strategic	Sustainability	Philanthropic		
1 Akenerji	4		1		2				
2 Akbank	2		1	3	3	1	18	1	1
3 Aksa Enerji	3		1						
4 Anadolu Efes	3			1	2	4	1		
5 Arçelik	4			1					
6 Aselsan	3								
7 Coca Cola Turkey	3		1		1	2		2	2
8 Doğuş Otomotive	3		2	3				2	
9 Ereğli Iron-Steel	3		1			1		3	1
10 Ford Otosan	3		1					3	2
11 İş Bank	4	1	1	2	2	1	3		1
12 Logo Software	2								
13 Migros Trade	4	2	1	3	1	2	1	6	
14 Otokar	3	1			1	1	1	2	
15 Polisan Holding	4		1		10	1	2	3	
16 Sabancı Holding	4		1	2		1	1		
17 Sişecam Holding	4		2		4	1		1	
18 Soda Industry	4							2	
19 T. Halk Bank	3	1						4	
20 Tofaş Otomotive	4	1			1	2	1	1	
21 Turkish Airlines	3		1			3	2		
22 Turkcell Com.	4			1	14			2	2
23 Ülker Biscuits	3		2		1				
24 Vakıflar Bank	3	9	1		2				
25 Yapı Kredi Bank	4		1	4	2	4		1	
	85	15	18	20	45	24	30	31	9

Table 4.4 Independent T-test results for age and foreign investment

	Age	N	Mean	Standard deviation	T	p
Collaborations	Companies ≤ 55	13	1,9538	1,34450	−1,162	,517
	Companies > 55	12	2,6000	1,43717		
	Foreign investment					
	Local companies	17	2,2824	1,60321	,94	,101
	Companies with foreign investment	8	2,2250	,91613		

companies form partnerships with NGOs mostly for *philanthropic* projects (20) followed by *sustainability* (18) and *strategic* projects (15). On the other hand, companies' *strategic* membership (45) outnumbers *philanthropic* (30) and *sustainability* (24) memberships.

Finally, to answer the second research question, an independent t-test is used. T-test analyses show no variance in business–NGO collaborations in terms of age and foreign investment (see Table 4.4).

Discussion

The BOP approach offers profit generation through answering the needs of the low-income population (Kolk et al., 2014; Prahalad, 2006). In this win-win scenario, the solutions to problems involved in entering new markets, through the introduction of new products that meet local needs, are complex and require collaborations with NGOs, governments, and other companies (Rodríguez, Giménez Thomsen, Arenas, & Pagell, 2016). Additionally, literature argues that businesses collaborate with NGOs more than other groups in transferring strategic resources and knowledge to create a better understanding of local market needs (Peloza & Falkenberg, 2009). Similarly, the collaborations formed between companies and NGOs arguably play a significant role in achieving sustainable development goals (Harangozó & Zilahy, 2015).

Along the same line, the current study focuses on understanding the forms of business–NGO collaborations that can have positive consequences in terms of the economic, ecologic, and social conditions of BOP in Turkey. Therefore, adopting the BOP approach, the sustainability reports of companies listed in the BIST Sustainability Index are analysed to identify the business–NGO collaborations that would improve the conditions of BOP. The study findings reveal five main forms of business–NGO collaborations. The first collaboration type is *partnership*, which has been discussed as an outstanding form of interaction, especially by studies on MNCs. A partnership offers opportunities to exchange competencies and the strengths of both companies and NGOs. For instance, companies can support NGO activities by offering financial and professional resources whereas NGOs can provide their core competencies of organizing and their expertise. Accordingly, the main motives for businesses to form partnerships with local NGOs for BOP are mostly to penetrate BOP markets and acquire resources (Calton, Werhane, Hartman, & Bevan, 2013; Hahn & Gold, 2014). Thus, companies have the advantage of lowering their risks of costs and failure when entering a new market. Studies also imply that a partnership with publicly known and trusted NGOs can boost firm legitimacy and improve firm reputation (Darko, 2014).

Another form revealed in the content analysis is *membership* for developing systematic dialogues related to strategic, sustainability, and philanthropic issues. Membership refers in particular to consultations and roundtable discussions helpful in receiving up-to-date information about the needs of BOP (Hart & Milstein, 2003; Kourula & Halme, 2008). For instance, Akbank is a member of various NGOs such as the Turkish Red Crescent Society, Poor's House, Make a Wish Association, Turkish Women Entrepreneurs Association, which specialise in answering BOP needs. These NGOs work at finding solutions to BOP problems and through becoming a member, companies support NGOs in increasing awareness or in providing financial resources for the given problems. Moreover, keeping dialogue through NGO membership is a critical information source through which businesses can understand the dynamics of BOP.

Within the context of the literature, the study findings show that business-NGO partnerships and memberships have subcategories: a) *strategic*, b) *sustainability*, and c) *philanthropic*. *Strategic partnerships* are formed with NGOs and are related to the core business activities of the companies examined. Similar to the previous studies, collaborations related to core business activities have the potential to create competitive advantage, as the focus of the collaborations relates to the company's own strategic intent (Lantos, 2001). In the study, for example, Halk Bank collaborates with the Turkish Exporters Assembly to offer sectorial solutions. Another example is the strategic membership of Şişe Group in the Ceramic, Glass, and Cement Raw Material Manufacturers Association. Şişe Group is one of the leading glass producers in Turkey and the given membership aligns with the company strategy of engaging in industry-related dialogue and contributing to industrial developments.

Secondly, as the number of NGOs that work for sustainability developments in Turkey increases, collaborations between sustainability NGOs and companies increase as well. Thereby, a new subcategory has emerged in the study in line with these newly developed sustainability NGOs. Interactions between companies and NGOs like Environment Protection Foundation, Sustainable Development Association, and Sustainability Academy are coded as *sustainability partnership* and *membership*. From the company's perspective, both strategic and sustainability projects can have positive outcomes, such as eco-efficiency and operational efficiency (Hockerts, 2015). For instance, Ford Otosan, an automobile company, has partnered with WWF Turkey to participate in the Green Office Programme and set up a 'green office team'. Similarly, operating in the brewery industry, Anadolu Efes reported that it is a member of the Sustainable Development Association. The Sustainable

Development Association (SDA) works to create awareness of sustainable development within the framework of the United Nation's Sustainable Development Goals in the Turkish business environment. To that end, SDA organises seminars and meetings related to carbon markets, sustainable agriculture methods, or women's employment. Therefore through membership, SDA establishes connection between companies to create a more sustainable business circle.

The third type of subcollaboration category revealed in the reports is *philanthropic partnership* and *membership*, which has no connection to a company's business operations. For this type of collaboration, the goal is to provide social help to those who need it. In the case of philanthropic-based collaborations, the degree of collaboration is limited mostly to economic support. For instance, İş bank provided financial support to the Turkish Chess Association so that children under legal protection can learn to play chess. Another example is İş bank and the Darüşşafaka Society's collaboration for the 81 Cities 81 Students project. The Darüşşafaka Society provides educational opportunities to children who have lost their fathers. Through the project, Isbank paid the education expenses of 81 students who succeeded at the Darüşşafaka's exams. Similarly, many of the companies examined are members of well-known civil society organizations (such as the Turkish Red Crescent, Turkish Volunteers for Education, and the Turkish Education Foundation) that work to provide solutions to social problems. Also, it has been found that Turkish companies form partnerships mostly for philanthropic activities ($n=20$), followed by sustainability ($n=18$) and strategic reasons ($n=15$). The previous studies indicate that philanthropy merged with traditions and religion form the basis of Turkish companies' corporate social responsibility practices (Alakavuklar, Kılıçaslan, & Öztürk, 2009). Turkish business groups that play a fundamental role in social and economic development of the country also play a pioneering role in the spread of corporate social responsibility activities through their foundations, established mainly for organizing philanthropic activities (Alakavuklar et al., 2009). Within this historical context and with the intention of creating a responsible social image, the philanthropic-based business-NGO partnerships are found to be the most common form of collaboration for Turkish businesses-NGOs. Yet, this is not the case for membership, as the highest number of memberships belongs to the strategic membership category ($n=45$). Strategic membership seeks to develop systematic industrial dialogues for increased operational ecoefficiency and effectiveness as well as sustained legitimacy for businesses (Harangozó & Zilahy, 2015). Being a member of an NGO that is related to the core business activities can also have normative and mimetic pressures compared to being a member of an NGO specialising in social problems.

Another way to provide economic support to BOP is through *sponsorships and donations* that companies provide to NGOs. From a business perspective, sponsorships and donations are also tools for increasing brand value and reputation (Kourula & Halme, 2008), though the previous studies have criticised them for their short-term or limited contribution to alleviating poverty (London, 2008). Yet donations offer economic support to increase the social and ecological life quality of BOP. From the ecological mindset, it is argued that BOP populations reside in places that are less costly and that have a low-quality infrastructure with polluted air and water. Within this framework, as the company with the highest number of donations, Migros' financial support to the WWF and the Aegean Forest Foundation to decrease air pollution can be given as an example. This donation would help reduce pollution in places where BOP populations mostly live. Another donation that Migros made to the Foundation for the Training and Protection of Mentally Handicapped Children can also help create better opportunities for poor families with disabled children.

Another category of business–NGO collaboration revealed in the study is *standards and certificates* related to NGOs such as the Global Reporting Initiative or ISO, which seeks to design global codes of conduct for responsible business practices. Moreover, these standard-setter NGOs can function as controlling mechanisms for company performance (Perez-Aleman & Sandilands, 2008). In this study, the findings reveal that Turkish companies collaborate with NGOs mostly to follow or adopt standards or certificates (collaboration $n = 85$). For instance, most of the examined companies state that they prepare their sustainability reports by following global reporting initiative reporting guidelines, participate in the Carbon Disclosure Programme, and report procedures to fight climate change. Moreover, most companies list their certificates for quality management, environmental management, and occupational health and safety. Additionally, they declare that they have certificates that are specific to their industry, as in the case of Anadolu Efes' adoption of Food Safety Management System standards (HACCP) as a beverage company. Accordingly, answering stakeholder expectations, legitimising business operations, and presenting a sustainable corporate image can be the reasons why Turkish companies are found to engage mostly with NGOs that develop standards of sustainability or give certifications. On the other hand, although this kind of engagement does not directly target BOP markets, sustainability codes of conduct that affect BOP can be critical in achieving improved social and working conditions, better salaries, better natural resources, less discrimination, and, thus, lessen social exclusion.

Previous studies indicate that initiatives providing self-financed growth (London, 2008) and approaching people at BOP as co-inventors or entrepreneurs of BOP initiatives (Simanis & Hart, 2009) are the key factors in poverty alleviation. The examined reports found only nine cases in which new ideas, products, or services are designed to meet the needs of BOP populations. These collaborations are coded as *social innovations*, as they aim to improve the conditions of people at BOP by offering permanent solutions. An example of this type of collaboration is Akbank's cooperation with the Endeavor Association to develop an entrepreneurship ecosystem by offering education and microcredits to young entrepreneurs for income generation and self-financed growth. Another social innovation engagement is the empowerment of women to participate in the labour force, designed by the Anadolu Group Foundation and Coca-Cola Turkey. Although all these projects offer long-term solutions to BOP populations' needs, this type of collaboration is limited, as only six companies reported *social innovation* in their sustainability reports. This finding also indicates that the examined Turkish companies do not evaluate BOP as partners in developing new business models or services. Accordingly, it can also be suggested that companies are not actively focused on solutions to alleviate the poverty and social exclusion that BOP experience.

The previous studies also provide evidence that, as interaction with global companies and the degree of internationalisation increases, the pressure on Turkish companies for sustainable and responsible business operations increases as well (Ozdora-Aksak & Atakan-Duman, 2016). Moreover, sustainability NGOs along with the BIST Sustainability Index are normative pressure tools for ideal business practices. Within this context, t-test analyses are conducted to determine whether there is a difference in collaborations between local companies and companies with foreign investment. However, no difference is found between local companies and companies with foreign investment. This finding indicates that local companies feel the same pressure to be sustainable, as they are also subjected to same stakeholder expectations. Additionally, this finding aligns with studies that prove many BOP initiatives are developed by small, local companies rather than by multinational companies (Kolk et al, 2014).

Conclusion

The first two targets of the United Nations' Sustainable Development Goals are to stop poverty and to stop hunger by 2030 (UN, 2019). The United Nations calls on all nations and companies to take responsibility and prepare action plans for poverty alleviation for sustainable development (e.g. Business Call to Action, an alliance set by UN for companies to generate business models for enhancing BOP conditions). Similarly, studies provide evidence that companies cannot ignore BOP needs to ensure sustainable growth. Yet the companies that design products/services to meet BOP markets have, until now, seemed limited.

In their efforts to address BOP needs, companies must cooperate with other stakeholders for resources. NGOs are among the most partnered stakeholders for companies in terms of resource acquisition and expertise transfer. Thus, within the BOP perspective, companies must collaborate with NGOs to enhance the results of increased profits and efficient operations, as well as to penetrate new markets and develop a stronger brand value.

The current study supports previous literature on the types of business-NGO collaborations. The emergence of subcategories is also meaningful in terms of Elkington's (1997) triple-bottom-line performance perspective. The study findings show that the partnership and membership collaboration types are related to strategic, sustainability, and social issues. In addition to membership and partnerships; standards and certificates, donations and sponsorships, and social innovations are found out as business–NGO collaboration types in the current study. Additionally, the positive outcomes for BOP of the given collaborations can be better income generation, better social and economic conditions, better working conditions and salaries, and the acquisition of social and economic support for their needs. However, the study results indicate that companies are not actively engaged with either finding permanent poverty alleviation solutions or meeting the needs of disadvantaged groups. According to the findings, companies collaborated mostly with NGOs to gain standards and certificates that would polish their responsible corporate image and reputation.

Thus, it is suggested that policy makers and managers concentrate more on ways to address BOP needs and alleviate poverty in Turkey. To encourage businesses to understand BOP dynamics, some governmental incentives or award mechanisms can be offered. Additionally, subsequent studies should question the means of accelerating interactions between businesses and NGOs along with other third parties for poverty alleviation. Also, for future studies, it is advised that interviews be conducted with top management to obtain an understanding of managerial attitudes and awareness of BOP needs and market in Turkey.

References

Adaman, F., & Keyder, Ç. (2006). Türkiye'de büyük kentlerin gecekondu ve çöküntü mahallelerinde yaşanan yoksulluk ve sosyal dışlanma. Retrieved from https://ec.europa.eu/employment_social/social_inclusion/docs/2006/study_turkey_tr.pdf

Alakavuklar, O. N., Kılıçaslan, S., & Öztürk, E. B. (2009). Türkiye'de Hayirseverlikten Kurumsal Sosyal Sorumluluğa Geçis: Bir Kurumsal Değişim Öyküsü. *Journal of Management Research, 9*(2), 103–143.

Albornoz, F., Cole, M. A., Elliott, R. J., & Ercolani, M. G. (2009). In search of environmental spillovers. *World Economy, 32*(1), 136–163. doi: 10.1111/j.1467-9701. 2008.01160.x

Ararat, M. (2008). A development perspective for 'corporate social responsibility': case of Turkey. *Corporate Governance: The International Journal of Business in Society, 8*(3), 271–285. https://doi.org/10.1108/14720700810879169

Arya, B., & Salk, J. (2006). Cross sector alliance learning and effectiveness of voluntary codes of corporate social responsibility. *Business Ethics Quarterly, 16* (2), 211–234. https://doi.org/10.5840/beq200616223

Ashman, D. (2001). Civil society collaboration with business: bringing empowerment back in. *World Development, 29*(7), 1097–1113. https://doi.org/10.1016/S0305-750X(01)00027-4

Atkinson, A. B. (2003). Multidimensional deprivation: contrasting social welfare and counting approaches. *The Journal of Economic Inequality, 1*(1), 51–65. https://doi.org/10.1023/A:1023903525276

Barry, B. M. (1998). Social exclusion, social isolation and the distribution of income. Retrieved from: http://eprints.lse.ac.uk/6516/1/Social_Exclusion,_Social_Isolation_and_the_Distribution_of_Income.pdf

Bendell, J. (2000). Civil regulation: a new form of democratic governance for the global economy. In Jem Bendell (Ed.), *Terms of Endearment: Business, NGOs and Sustainable Development* (pp. 239–254). Sheffield, UK: Greenleaf Publishing. https://doi.org/10.4324/9781351282727

Bonn, I. and Fisher, J. (2011). Sustainability: the missing ingredient in strategy. *Journal of Business Strategy, 32*(1), 5–14. https://doi.org/10.1108/02756661111100274

Byiers, B., Guadagno, F., & Karaki, K. (2015). From looking good to doing good: mapping CSO-business partnerships. Retrieved from: http://ecdpm.org/wp-content/uploads/DP-182-Mapping-CSO-Business-Partnerships-ECDPM-2015.pdf

Calton, J. M., Werhane, P. H., Hartman, L. P., & Bevan, D. (2013). Building partnerships to create social and economic value at the base of the global development pyramid. *Journal of Business Ethics, 117*(4), 721–733. https://doi.org/10.1007/s10551-013-1716-0

Christensen, L. T., Morsing, M., & Thyssen, O. (2017). License to critique: a communication perspective on sustainability standards. *Business Ethics Quarterly, 27*(2), 239–262. https://doi.org/10.1017/beq.2016.66

Cormier, D., Magnan, M., & Van Velthoven, B. (2005). Environmental disclosure quality in large German companies: economic incentives, public pressures or institutional conditions?. *European Accounting Review, 14*(1), 3–39. https://doi.org/10.1080/0963818042000339617

Cutcliffe, J. R., & McKenna, H. P. (1999). Establishing the credibility of qualitative research findings: the plot thickens. *Journal of Advanced Nursing, 30*(2), 374–380. https://doi.org/10.1046/j.1365-2648.1999.01090.x

Darko, E. (2014). Private sector and NGO engagement: descriptive list of the main ways the private sector and NGOs currently collaborate in development work. Retrieved from: https://assets.publishing.service.gov.uk/media/57a089eee5274a27b2000325/Private_Sector_and_NGO_Engagement.pdf

Deeming, C. & Gubhaju, B. (2014). The mis-measurement of extreme global poverty: a case study in the Pacific Islands. *Journal of Sociology, 51*(3): 689–706. https://doi.org/10.1177/1440783314523867

Desa, G., & Koch, J. L. (2014). Scaling social impact: building sustainable social ventures at the base-of-the-pyramid. *Journal of Social Entrepreneurship, 5*(2), 146–174. https://doi.org/10.1080/19420676.2013.871325

Dyllick, T., & Hockerts, K. (2002). Beyond the business case for corporate sustainability. *Business Strategy and the Environment, 11*(2): 130–141. https://doi.org/10.1002/bse.323

Elkington, J. (1997). *Cannibals With Forks – Triple Bottom Line of 21st Century Business.* Stoney Creek, CT: New Society Publishers.

Elo, S., Kääriäinen, M., Kanste, O., Pölkki, T., Utriainen, K., & Kyngäs, H. (2014). Qualitative content analysis: a focus on trustworthiness. *SAGE Open, 4*(1), 2158244014522633. https://doi.org/10.1177/2158244014522633

Gereffi, G., Garcia-Johnson, R., & Sasser, E. (2001). The NGO-industrial complex. *Foreign Policy,* (125), 56. Retrieved from: https://elibrary.ru/item.asp?id=4274345

Gold, S., Hahn, R., & Seuring, S. (2013). Sustainable supply chain management in 'Base of the Pyramid' food projects – a path to triple bottom line approaches for multinationals? *International Business Review, 22*(5), 784–799. https://doi.org/10.1016/j.ibusrev.2012.12.006

Hahn, R., & Gold, S. (2014). Resources and governance in 'base of the pyramid'-partnerships: assessing collaborations between businesses and non-business actors. *Journal of Business Research, 67*(7), 1321–1333. https://doi.org/10.1016/j.jbusres.2013.09.002

Hammond, A. L., Kramer, W. J., Katz, R. S., Tran, J. T., & Walker, C. (2007). The next 4 billion. *Innovations: Technology, Governance, Globalization, 2*(1–2), 147–158. http://www.wri.org/publication/the-next-4-billion.

Harangozó, G., & Zilahy, G. (2015). Cooperation between business and non-governmental organizations to promote sustainable development. *Journal of Cleaner Production, 89,* 18–31. https://doi.org/10.1016/j.jclepro.2014.10.092

Hart, S. L., & Milstein, M. B. (2003). Creating sustainable value. *Academy of Management Perspectives, 17*(2), 56–67. https://doi.org/10.5465/ame.2003.10025194

Hartman, C. L., Hofman, P. S., & Stafford, E. R. (1999). Partnerships: a path to sustainability. *Business Strategy and the Environment, 8*(5), 255–266. https://doi.org/10.1002/(SICI)1099-0836

Hickey, G., & Kipping, E. (1996). A multi-stage approach to the coding of data from open-ended questions. *Nurse Researcher, 4,* 81–91. https://doi.org/10.7748/nr.4.1.81.s9

Hockerts, K. (2015). A cognitive perspective on the business case for corporate sustainability. *Business Strategy and the Environment, 24*(2), 102–122. https://doi.org/10.1002/bse.1813

Karadağ, M. A., & Saraçoğlu, B. (2015). Çok Boyutlu Yoksulluk Analizi: Türkiye-AB Karşılaştırması. *Amme Idaresi Dergisi, 48*(4).

Kolk, A. (2008). Sustainability, accountability and corporate governance: exploring multinationals' reporting practices. *Business Strategy and the Environment, 17*(1), 1–15. https://doi.org/10.1002/bse.511

Kolk, A., Rivera-Santos, M., & Rufín, C. (2014). Reviewing a decade of research on the 'base/bottom of the pyramid' (BOP) concept. *Business & Society, 53*(3), 338–377. https://doi.org/10.1177/0007650312474928

Kong, N., Salzmann, O., Steger, U., & Ionescu-Somers, A. (2002). Moving business/industry towards sustainable consumption: the role of NGOs. *European Management Journal, 20*(2), 109–127. https://doi.org/10.1016/S0263-2373(02)00022-1

Kourula, A. (2006). Stakeholder identification and engagement – nongovernmental organizations as corporate stakeholders. *Electronic Proceedings of European Business Ethics Network (EBEN) Annual Conference on 'Ethics in and of Global Organizations',* Vienna, Austria, September, 21–23.

Kourula, A., & Halme, M. (2008). Types of corporate responsibility and engagement with NGOs: an exploration of business and societal outcomes. *Corporate Governance: The International Journal of Business in Society, 8*(4), 557–570. https://doi.org/10.1108/14720700810899275

Krippendorff K. (1980). *Content Analysis: An Introduction to Its Methodology.* Sage Publications, Newbury Park.

Krippendorff, K. (1989). Content analysis. In E. Barnouw, G. Gerbner, W. Schramm, T. L. Worth, & L. Gross (Eds), *International Encyclopaedia of Communication,* Vol. 1, 403–407. New York, NY: Oxford University Press. Retrieved from http://repository.upenn.edu/asc_papers/226

Lantos, G. P. (2001). The boundaries of strategic corporate social responsibility. *Journal of Consumer Marketing, 18*(2), 595–630. https://doi.org/10.1108/07363760110410281

Li, N., Toppinen, A., Tuppura, A., Puumalainen, K., & Hujala, M. (2011). Determinants of sustainability disclosure in the global forest industry. *EJBO: Electronic Journal of Business Ethics and Organizational Studies, 16*(1), 33–40.

Limanli, Ö. (2017, January). Multidimensional poverty in Turkey. In *Turkish Economic Association International Conference on Economics 2016*. Turkish Economy Institution.

London, T. (2008, August). The base-of-the-pyramid perspective: a new approach to poverty alleviation. *Academy of Management Proceedings* (Vol. 2008(1) 1, pp. 1–6). Briarcliff Manor, NY 10510: Academy of Management. https://doi.org/10.5465/ambpp.2008.33716520

Malmborg, Å., & Mark-Herbert, C. (2010).ISO 14001 certification in BoP markets. *Greener Management International, 56*, 57–73. http://www.jstor.org/stable/greemanainte.56.57.

Milne M. J., & Adler, W.A. (1999). Exploring the reliability of social and environmental disclosures content analysis. *Accounting, Auditing & Accountability Journal, 12*(2), 237–256. https://doi.org/10.1108/09513579910270138

Martens, K. (2002). Mission impossible? Defining nongovernmental organizations. *International Journal of Voluntary and Non-profit Organizations, 13*(3), 271–285. https://doi.org/10.1023/A:1020341526691

Meng, X, Zeng S, & Tam, C. (2013). From voluntarism to regulation: a study on ownership, economic performance and corporate environmental information disclosure in China. *Journal of Business Ethics, 116*(1), 217–232. https://doi.org/10.1007/s10551-012-1462-8

Michelon, G. (2011). Sustainability disclosure and reputation: a comparative study. *Corporate Reputation Review, 14*(2), 79–96. https://doi.org/10.1057/crr.2011.10

Mohr J. J., Sengupta S., & Slater, S.F. (2012). Serving base-of-the-pyramid markets: meeting real needs through a customised approach. *Journal of Business Strategy, 33*(6), 4–14. https://doi.org/10.1108/02756661211281453

Monzer, D. A., Rebs, T., Khalid, R. U., & Brandenburg, M. (2018). Sustainable supply chain management at the base of pyramid: a literature review. *Social and Environmental Dimensions of Organizations and Supply Chains* (pp. 235–257). Cham: Springer. https://doi.org/10.1007/978-3-319-59587-0_14

Mulgan, G., Ali, R., Halkett, R., & Sanders, B. (2007, September). *In and Out of Sync: The Challenge of Growing Social Innovations (Research Report)*. London, England: National Endowment for Science, Technology and the Arts. https://ci.nii.ac.jp/naid/20000735184/en/

Overdevest, C. (2004). Codes of conduct and standard setting in the forest sector: constructing markets for democracy. *Industrial Relations, 59*(1): 172–195. https://doi.org/10.7202/009131ar

Ozdora-Aksak, E., & Atakan-Duman, S. (2016). Gaining legitimacy through CSR: an analysis of Turkey's 30 largest corporations. *Business Ethics: A European Review, 25*(3), 238–257. https://doi.org/10.1111/beer.12114

Peloza, J., & Falkenberg, L. (2009). The role of collaboration in achieving corporate social responsibility objectives. *California Management Review, 51*(3), 95–113.

Perez-Aleman, P., & Sandilands, M. (2008). Building value at the top and the bottom of the global supply chain: MNC-NGO partnerships. *California Management Review, 51*(1), 24–49.

Prahalad, C. K. (2006). *The Fortune at the Bottom of the Pyramid*. Upper Saddle River, NJ: Wharton School Pub.

Prahalad, C. K. (2012). Bottom of the pyramid as a source of breakthrough innovations. *Journal of Product Innovation Management, 29*(1), 6–12. https://doi.org/10.1111/j.1540-5885.2011.00874.x

Prahalad, C. K., & Hammond, A. (2002). Serving the world's poor, profitably. *Harvard Business Review, 80*(9), 48–59.

Prahalad, C. K., and Hart, S. (2002). The fortune at the bottom of the pyramid. *Strategy and Business, 26*(44), 54–67.

Porter, M. and Kramer M.R. (2007). Strategy and society: the link between competitive advantage and corporate social responsibility. *Harvard Business Review, 48*(12), 78–94. https://doi.org/10.1108/sd.2007.05623ead.006

Porter, M. and Kramer, M. (2011). Creating shared value. *Harvard Business Review, 89*(1/2), 62–77.

Rivera-Santos, M., Rufin, C., & Kolk, A. (2012). Bridging the institutional divide: partnerships in subsistence markets. *Journal of Business Research, 65*(12), 1721–1727. https://doi.org/10.1016/j.jbusres.2012.02.013

Rodríguez, J. A., Giménez Thomsen, C., Arenas, D., & Pagell, M. (2016). NGOs' initiatives to enhance social sustainability in the supply chain: poverty alleviation through supplier development programs. *Journal of Supply Chain Management, 52*(3), 83–108. https://doi.org/10.1111/jscm.12104

Qi, G., Zeng, S., Yin, H., & Lin, H. (2013). ISO and OHSAS certifications: how stakeholders affect corporate decisions on sustainability. *Management Decision, 51*(10), 1983–2005. https://doi.org/10.1108/MD-11-2011-0431

Simanis, E., & Hart, S. (2011). Innovation from the inside out. *MIT Sloan Management Review,* 9–18.

Starik, M., & Kanashiro, P. (2013). Toward a theory of sustainability management: uncovering and integrating the nearly obvious. *Organization & Environment, 26*(1), 7–30. https://doi.org/10.1177/1086026612474958

Turkish Statistical Institute (TSI). (2015). *Poverty Statistics.* Retrieved from: http://www.tuik.gov.tr/PreHaberBultenleri.do?id=21867

Turkish Statistical Institute (TSI). (2018). *International Economic Indicators.* Retrieved from: http://tuik.gov.tr/UstMenu.do?metod=istgosterge

Unerman, J., & O'Dwyer, B. (2010). NGO accountability and sustainability issues in the changing global environment. *Public Management Review, 12*(4), 475–486. https://doi.org/10.1080/14719037.2010.496258

United Nations (2019). *The Sustainable Development Goals Report 2019.* New York: UN. Retrieved from: https://unstats.un.org/sdgs/report/2019/The-Sustainable-Development-Goals-Report-2019.pdf

United Nations Development Programme. (2018). *Human Development Indices and Indicators.* Retrieved from: http://hdr.undp.org/sites/default/files/2018_human_development_statistical_update.pdf

Yurdakul, D., Atik, D., & Dholakia, N. (2017). Redefining the bottom of the pyramid from a marketing perspective. *Marketing Theory, 17*(3), 289–303. https://doi.org/10.1177/1470593117704265

Webb, J. W., Kistruck, G. M., Ireland, R. D., & Ketchen Jr, D. J. (2010). The entrepreneurship process in base of the pyramid markets: the case of multinational enterprise/nongovernment organization alliances. *Entrepreneurship Theory and Practice, 34*(3), 555–581. http://dx.doi.org/10.1111/j.1540-6520.2009.00349.x

World Bank. (October, 2018). *Poverty and Equity Brief: Turkey.* Retrieved from: http://povertydata.worldbank.org/poverty/country/TUR

Part IV

Design, integration, innovation, and change of BOP markets

5 Systemic constraints to financial inclusion in Bangladesh and recommended solutions

Sajid Amit and Lumbini Barua

Introduction

Ready-made garments (RMG) manufacturing for export in Bangladesh has been creating huge momentum in the employment sector since 1980, creating opportunities for a large number of people to work in this industry (Ainul, Hossain, Amin, & Rob, 2013). The RMG workers in Bangladesh are predominantly female coming from poor economic backgrounds. Concurrently, with about 65.0% of the unbanked population of the country being female (Demirgüç-Kunt, Klapper, Singer, Ansar, & Hess, 2017), the RMG sector comes to attention as a unique area for promoting financial inclusion. In this context, both government and non-government sectors have initiated manifold interventions like microfinance, agent banking, mobile banking, fintech, etc. for including female RMG workers in the formal financial system. Most of the female RMG workers earn around $2.5–4.0 per day, which, as per World Bank definitions, places them squarely within the base of the economic pyramid (Hammond, Kramer, Katz, Tran, & Walker, 2007).

Among the said interventions, agent banking has been being deployed by formal financial institutions such as banks with a view to bringing banking services to the doorstep of the excluded and marginalised peoples. Agent banking met with impressive success in many cases, but evidence suggest that there are still multifaceted challenges existing in the process of financial inclusion of the RMG workers occurring both from the supply side and the demand side. While some research findings emphasise the lack of awareness among the unbanked population, considering it as the major constraint in financial inclusion (TP, 2014), research is being focused on determing the constraints prevailing in the supply side as well (Damodaran, 2012).

The objective of this study was to highlight the barriers of financial inclusion of the RMG workers in Bangladesh through agent banking services led by commercial banks. While this research identified miscellaneous obstacles existing, a greater portion of these challenges was found to exist with the supply side, i.e., the commercial banks. By assesing the results of a pilot project implemebted by Swisscontact South Asia Regional Office (SARO), the study identifies the systemic constraints pertaining to banks' deployment of agent banking, especially with regard to its set-up and roll-out; account opening and usage; product development and financial literacy programmes. Agent banking is known as business correspondent banking more widely, and has become a ways and means for private commercial banks to enter the space of micro lending and lending to the Bottom of the Pyramid (BOP). The model is growing in Bangaldesh, as it has been doing in other developing countries as well (Mas & Siedek, 2008; Ho, 2017).

Background

Financial inclusion through banking sector outreach can ensure that all members of a society can avail their required financial services at a fair price, at the right place, in the right form, at the right time, and without facing any sort of discrimination (Aro-Gordon, 2016). The objective of financial inclusion is to include the out-of-reach and disadvantaged section of the society in the formal financial system (Aduda & Kalunda, 2012). This chapter sheds light on the existing condition of access to financial services of ready-made garments (RMG) workers by assessing data from a donor-funded project known as Sarathi, implemented by Swisscontact.[1] The four major areas of intervention for Sarathi are financial literacy programmes; product development; agent banking[2] set-up and roll-out; and bank account opening and usage. This chapter recognises these intervention areas as the key areas in case of research about financial inclusion of the RMG sector in Bangladesh. By assessing the success, failure, and findings of the said project, this chapter underscores the existing systemic challenges both in the banking and non-banking sector for identifying the hindering factors with the hope of mitigating barriers to financial inclusion in Bangladesh. This chapter also presents some recommendations based on the findings of the research.

Methodology

This study followed a descriptive research approach, predominantly employing qualitative tools and techniques. For this study, focus group discussion (FGD) and key informant interview (KII) were used for data collection. Focus group discussion has been recognised as an efficacious tool for explaining attitude of the consumers and also for elucidating a better understanding of the area of interest in hand (Mishra, 2016). Although FGD can be used as a unilateral methodology for qualitative research, complementing FGD with another tool like one-to-one qualitative interview has been recommended by researchers for triangulation purpose (Boateng, 2012). For this reason, this study has adopted both FGD and KII as research tools with a view to enabling greater absorption of the research area. Four FGDs were conducted with the RMG workers from the target groups of the two partner banks (two FGDs each for two commercial banks); each FGD consisting of 10–12 participants. The participants of the FGDs were nominated by the banks and included vendors who were responsible for training their agents as well as senior and mid-level banking staff. Four KIIs were conducted with the agents of the banks (two KIIs with each bank) and two more KIIs with the banks' full-time staff (one KII with each bank). The participants of these interviews were selected using convenience sampling technique which is a commonly used method of sampling FGD participants (Dawson, Manderson, & Tallo, 1993). The time constraint of the RMG workers was the compelling reason for using convenience sampling. This study also made use of data collected through discussions with project staff and review of project documents.

In this research, an inductive approach to analysis of qualitative data has been used. This is a particularly useful approach to analyse qualitative data, especially when the goal is both to uncover patterns that frequently occur in the raw data and to use the qualitative data for policy prescriptions via a model that can be explained using a handful of primary categories of findings (Bryman & Burgess, 1994; Thomas, 2006). This is often called a general inductive approach. A specific set of objectives usually guide such approaches (Dey, 1993), and in this case, the objective is to uncover strategies for the expansion of agent banking or business correspondent banking in the context of Bangladesh.

Using thematic analysis (Braun & Clarke, 2006), the qualitative data collected from the FGDs and KIIs were analysed and the four themes considered were in line with the four major intervention areas of this project (financial literacy programmes, product development, agent banking set-up and roll-out, and bank account opening and usage). These themes coincide with the impact criteria of the pilot project. The quotes from the collected data through the FGDs and KIIs were coded and then compiled and sorted under the predetermined themes and were presented in narrative manner (see Table 5.1 in the Appendix for the details of the codes).

Literature review

According to the 2017 Global Findex Database, about 69.0% of adults across the globe have a bank account (The World Bank, nd). However, 1.7 billion adults still lack an account at any financial institution. Unfortunately, nearly half of these unbanked world population live in just seven countries with developing economies: Bangladesh (3.0%), China, India, Indonesia, Mexico, Nigeria, and Pakistan. Women are further deprived of financial inclusion through banking as nearly 56.0% of the unbanked populations globally are women. Thus, the gender gap among the banked population remains constant at 9 percentage points (Demirgüç-Kunt et al., 2017).

In case of progress in gaining account ownership in Bangladesh, partial progress has been achieved since 2011 as the inclusion was stagnated among women. In 2017, 50.0% of adults owned a transaction account and among them only 36.0% were women. In addition, 65.0% of unbanked adults in Bangladesh are women. There is also a significant gap in account ownership between richer and poorer section of the population, which is 17 percentage points (Demirgüç-Kunt et al., 2017).

In this context, the microfinance institutions have been acting as the driving force of financial inclusion for a long time. However, due to the high cost of setting up banks, and an ever changing complex and digitally oriented ecosystem, the banks have been forced to leave behind the hard-to-reach customers. Fortunately, the digital financial services (DFS), especially the agent banking services and mobile financial services (MFS), constitute a silver lining and are expected to enable banks to reach the last-mile customers (Amit, 2017). In Bangladesh, the share of mobile money accounts has increased from 3.0% to 21.0% since 2011 (Demirgüç-Kunt et al., 2017).

Estimates by Accenture, a global management consulting and professional services firm, suggest that banks could generate annual revenue of about US$110 billion by 2020 within emerging markets globally by including unbanked adults into the formal financial system while raising their financial services spending levels on average to that of lower middle-income countries. For Bangladesh, the revenue potential is estimated to be US$2.3 billion (Accenture and Care International, 2015). According to Bangladesh Bank data, the number of agent banking accounts in Bangladesh more than doubled in 2017 within one year with 12,14,000 accounts. Thus, the experts in Bangladesh recognises agent banking as the most effective tool for financial inclusion of the extreme poor in Bangladesh (*The Daily Star*, 2018).

In fact, there is a growing body of academic literature on the business opportunity for for-profit organizations at the bottom-of-the-pyramid. There is a meta-analysis on various organizations' business performance with regard to customers at the BOP that highlights the extensive list of authors (Kolk, Rivera-Santos, & Rufin, 2014). This is partially driven by the growing number of development interventions, projects funded by aid agencies and implemented by NGOs that focus on 'market-based interventions' and often partner with for-profit companies to create distribution networks to access the BOP customer (Tasavori, Ghauri, & Zaefarian, 2014).

The target group of the financial inclusion project Sarathi is the RMG workers. They constitute for the banks a huge pool of potential customers who are currently out of the reach of the formal financial institutions and are predominantly female. According to the estimates of Bangladesh Bank, there are about 16 million bank accounts in Bangladesh. However, only 21,500 accounts belong to RMG workers (CARE Bangladesh, 2017).

According to the findings of research carried on by the Population Council and Levi Strauss Foundation on the existing savings practice among the female RMG workers, 28.0% of them saved with banks, 23.9% with insurance companies, 5.7% with NGOs, 13.6% with other people, 5.7% with their employers and 14.8% of them saved at home. Only 5.2% of their survey respondents were found to have a traditional bank account. Interestingly, the study respondents were not aware of the differences among bank savings, NGO savings, and insurance company savings (Ainul et al., 2013).

CARE Bangladesh, an international NGO working in Bangladesh, conducted a research on the current situation of financial inclusion of the female

RMG workers in Bangladesh. Their study revealed that among their respondents only 26.0% had bank accounts. Eighty-seven per cent of them used mobile money transfers but only 3.0% of them were bKash[3] account registered under their names. Three requirements of the female RMG workers were discovered through this research. Those are access to loans, bank and bKash account registered under their own names, and financial training. Another finding of the study was that a large portion of the female RMG workers did not have full control over their own earnings or salary. So, they can hugely benefit from financial services that provide them with greater management authority of their finances and greater savings (CARE Bangladesh, 2017).

Increasingly, over the last several years, owing to the digital transformation of financial institutions, and wider access of the internet among rural and BOP customers, there is a growing body of academic literature on how financial institutions can address the requirements of BOP customers (Berger & Nakata, 2013; Selvarajan, 2018). In the context of Bangladesh, there is limited academic research on this topic, as most of the research till date is focused on the impact of microfinance institutions (MFIs) (Akter, 2016). However, given the proliferation of business correspondent banking models in Bangladesh (referred to as agent banking locally), the research is a timely contribution (Alo, 2019; Islam, 2018). In the academic literature on business correspondent banking itself, there is often a distinction made between the demand and supply side of the intervention, and constraints thereof (Abrol, 2018). However, in this research, it is posited that the supply side (i.e., banks that supply financial services) have a greater onus on them to address systemic constraints in order to render agent banking more successful and cast a wider net on the unbanked peoples of Bangladesh. Although demand side constraints such as lack of financial literacy are an issue, there is evidence to suggest that financial literacy and the imparting of it should be undertaken by the supply side as well, in light of experiences of other countries attempting to drive financial inclusion (Gaisina & Kaidarova, 2017).

Findings of the study

This section presents the issues and challenges identified to be existing in the banking sector and among other stakeholders (e.g., beneficiaries, agents, and factory supervisors) that are hindering the process of financial inclusion of the RMG workers.

Systemic challenges in the banking sector

This chapter has identified several systemic challenges in the banks,[4] one of the primary stakeholders in driving financial inclusion, through interviews and discussions with the different groups of people affiliated with the project. Below are some of the major constraints found being generated from the structural issues, functions, attitudes, or aptitudes of the banks studied.

Banks' efforts towards sustaining agent banking

Without setting up a separate agent banking division, the effectiveness and sustainability of this sector are expected to become compromised. For instance, Dutch-Bangla Bank, a popular commercial bank in Bangladesh, has already created a separate agent banking department realising the potential of this sector (Dutch-Bangla Bank, n.d.). Unfortunately, this has not become a common practice in the banking sector yet, although after completing the pilot phase, both banks considered in this project showed interest in treating the agent banking activities as a separate division. Moreover, Bank Asia[5] revealed their consideration about dedicating a separate Human Resources (HR) unit for agent banking. Similarly, NRBC bank[6] expressed that the pilot project changed their strategy of grouping the agent banking under their card division and they wanted to turn it into a new division. However, from the interviews and repeated discussions with the senior managements of both banks, it was appreciated that the banks require a bit more time and persuasion in order to properly respect and prioritise agent banking.

This means that the banks realise the potentialities of agent banking in generating customers among the unbanked. Treating agent banking only as corporate social responsibility (CSR) is not likely to ensure sustainability of this sector. The banks should realise the potentials of this target population to become regular clients of the banking services and products. It is therefore a significant enabling factor that the management bodies of the banks appear to be committed to including RMG workers in their customer base, with a view towards the long-term potential for business they are likely to generate.

Banks' attempts in product development and promotion
of the agent banking model

The banks are required to get the newly developed or modified products approved by members of their respective boards. Delays in product approval for the agent banking can harm the regular functioning of the sector. However, this process was found to be time-consuming. In fact, KIIs with the bank officials revealed that whenever the matter of approving products for the pilot project phase was raised in the meetings, it was ignored, shifting attention towards other issues. Given the newness of this potential business channel, such shortcomings are expected but to ensure regularity, in the long run the process of product approval should require less time.

Several studies on agent banking carried out in various countries suggest that consistent branding of agent banking and the agents is vital for attracting customers from the target group and incentivising the agents as well (Lehman, 2010; Santu, Mawanza, & Muredzi, 2017). However, findings from this study through the KIIs with the agents disclose that neither of the banks gave adequate effort in carrying out promotional campaigns for the RMG workers. During the assessment period, all the agents expressed that they felt the requirement of greater initiatives aimed towards building bridges between themselves and the RMG workers.

Conducting financial literacy programmes and appointing financial counsellors

In this pilot project, one of the banks (Bank Asia) relied on their regular staff for conducting financial literacy programmes. This approach was found to be challenging for the staff, as they did not have experience in speaking the language of the low-income people. On the other hand, the other bank which was part of the study (NRBC Bank) outsourced its literacy tasks to a specialised third party. This enabled the bank to dedicate more time and personnel while engaging with RMG workers. However, quality of the appointed counsellors is an important issue to consider for adopting this strategy.

An interesting finding from the FGDs of the RMG workers for this study was that, with regard to gender-sensitivity, selection of female financial counsellors plays a part in ensuring the success of the future literacy programmes. Feedback from the attendees suggests that a rigorous training of financial counsellors is important to ensure that they themselves are adequately informed of the knowledge they will be imparting to RMG workers.

However, KIIs with the bank officials suggest that there is a lack of incentives for the financial counsellors who conduct the literacy sessions for RMG workers. In most of the cases, the full-time employees of the banks were assigned as financial counsellors. As they were already preoccupied with other duties and responsibilities, their focus got compromised. Therefore, incentivising the financial counsellors duly is essential for ensuring better performance from them during the training sessions.

Complexity of registration and limitation of services through agent banking

According to the agents interviewed, the identification documents required for opening bank accounts are as follows: copy of educational certificates; national ID; trade licence; passport size photo; citizenship certificate; bank statement; and three references (e.g. from a banker, the chairman of the Union Parishad, or the headteacher of a high school). During FGDs with the RMG workers it was discovered that about seven respondents did not have a National Identification Document (NID), although this is one of the requirements for opening a bank account (ICT Division, 2015). The lack of appropriate documents has also been cited as a core constrained to account opening by operating agents. In the study by CARE Bangladesh, they also found that their respondents viewed the process of bank account opening as difficult and troublesome. Only 29.0% of the respondents shared that banking seems easy to them and probably due to these complexities, 45.0% of the respondents believed that they are required to be at least semi-literate to enter into a banking system (CARE Bangladesh, 2017).

Limitation of services available in the agent banking outlets can be considered as another significant constraint. The banks ought to increase the products and services offered through their agent banking to keep both their customers and agents properly incentivised (Lehman, 2010; Mwende, Bichanga, & Mosoti, 2015; Ndegwa, 2017; Parvez, Islam, & Woodard, 2015). If the agents cannot provide the customers with their required services, it will discourage them from availing of their services at all. On the other hand, without the ample number of products and services at their disposal, the agents can lose motivation due to the lack of opportunities of revenue generation. The most scalable revenue source for the agents is the amount of deposits that an agent outlet can mobilise. However, emphasis on additional services such as utility bills, account opening and withdrawals, fund transfer, loan disbursement, and collection, credit and debit card application can increase revenue streams for agents through generating volume of transactions and balancing liquidity (Lehman, 2010).

Banks' effort in persuading the potential customers

According to the FGD findings, female RMG workers are found to be far more comfortable approaching female agents. Unfortunately, very few agents available to banks are female. Women agents are found to build a comfort zone for the female customers while approaching and making use of agent banking services (Rahman, 2016; Thakur, Sahoo, Barooah, Sivalingam, & Njoroge, 2016). Thus, activities aimed towards the identification and development of female agents who could service RMG workers would constitute a significant milestone in the development of the agent banking industry.

Creating trust among the potential customers can be considered as one of the most significant issue for ensuring the growth of the agent banking industry (Lotto, 2016). According to the findings from the KIIs, confusion exists around the word 'agent' as most RMG workers do not understand the concept of how a bank can operate without its full physical structure. From the discussions with the Sarathi team it was revealed that some RMG workers questioned the security of their money as they felt that the agent outlets are not fully secured and can be subject to theft or robbery. Such scenarios mean that agent outlets are yet to gain the trust and confidence of RMG workers. Effective steps need to be taken to mitigate this obstacle.

Banks' overall treatment towards the agents

The Bangladesh Bank's agent banking guidelines mandate that agents are provided a reasonable fee/commission for the services they perform (Bangladesh Bank, 2013). Yet, this study found that there are significant differences among the banks relating to the fees and commissions paid to agents. Both of the partner banks were found to adopt their own different models and revenue streams for their respective agents. For instance, according to the agents interviewed, one of the partner banks (NRBC Bank) provided their agents with a 0.2% commission per transaction (cash-in/cash-out). The agents expressed that they were not satisfied with the mentioned amount.

Based on the FGD and KII findings, estimates from this study suggest that an agent for this pilot project would be profitable, if he or she were able to earn about US$213–261 per month. However, this was not found to be happening for most of the agents, therefore requiring cross-subsidy. Meanwhile, the agents expressed during the interviews that cross-subsidising agent banking with other businesses (e.g., rural electrification bill collection, mobile phone top-up, etc.) is required for agent banking to sustain in the present time. They further suggested that the trend of agents increasing engaged in utility bill payments, and the commission they receive, is likely to help offset near-term losses in agent banking.

The partner banks in this pilot project deployed less than sufficient staff to support the agents which led to lack of motivation among the agents. Moreover, trainings conducted for agents were non-residential in nature and were held at the head offices of respective banks, which required agents to commute long distances from their neighbourhoods, located on the outskirts of Dhaka city. According to the agents interviewed, the long commute and traffic congestions discouraged agents from attending training of longer duration thus further limiting their motivation and understanding of the agent banking model.

Capacity building of the agents is another crucial issue for sustaining agent banking. Frequent and mandatory training of the agents is recommended by most of the studies in this area (Afande & Mbuga, 2015; Hossain, Dey, & Afzal, 2015; Santu, Mawanza, & Muredzi, 2017). This study found from interviewing the bank officials that the agents lacked the capacity to carry out marketing and client acquisition tasks. They were unable to engage with clients meaningfully, which, to some extent, deterred the conversion of financial literacy and awareness about bank products into bank accounts. Therefore, further capacity building of agents through continuous training and underlining proper strategies to mitigate possible risks are some of the crucial requirements that must be in place prior to rolling out additional services through agents.

Other challenges

Creating necessary awareness among the deprived people about agent banking as a suitable option for them is absolutely crucial for financially including the excluded (Hossain, Dey, & Afzal, 2015; Mwende, Bichanga, & Mosoti, 2015). Both primary and secondary research suggests that there is a significant lack of awareness among the RMG workers regarding agent banking services and many of those who are aware are not entirely confident about the credibility of agents. Such conditions lead them to save their wages with landlords and local cooperative societies despite the fact that these alternative options remain outside the purview of the formal financial system.

It was comprehended from the FGDs with the RMG workers that the financial literacy sessions were well received by them and particularly by the female RMG workers. This suggests that there is a high requirement for increasing the frequency of the training sessions. However, interviews with banks and FGDs with RMG workers revealed that a standalone one-time financial literacy programme was not sufficient for the target group. This is because, during the lunch-time sessions, the workers were distracted, hungry, or had other personal priorities to tend to. FGD with the RMG workers manifested that a refresher session or several refresher sessions are required as just 50.0% of RMG workers claimed during FGDs that they partially remembered what was taught and only 30.0% remembered fully.

Another crucial obstacle discovered in the interviews is that the RMG factories' supervisors or floor in-charge personnel are found to pose serious constraints in delivering financial literacy trainings and other relevant operations of agent banking as well. They prevent the workers from joining the sessions. Furthermore, they lacked gender-sensitivity, respect for workers, and appreciation for the pilot intervention. It was reported that, while contacting the agents to open bank accounts, the RMG workers faced restriction and, sometimes, obstruction. In one interview with a partner bank it was expressed that certain floor-in-charge personnel tend to consider RMG workers as their property. Moreover, they are often hesitant to allow any activity that they perceive as a disturbance to the regular routine of other workers. This is why those factory personnel were considered as the single-most hindering factor to the success of the pilot project. Above all, it can be concluded that the floor-in-charge personnel can be a serious constraint to the growth and success of the promotion of agent banking among the RMG workers. It would be important to account for this and conceptualise activities that render them facilitators rather than inhibitors to the financial inclusion of RMG workers.

From the discussion above, it can be viewed that there are some significant challenges existing among the stakeholders other than the banks in the process of financial inclusion of the RMG sector. However, it is clearly evident that most of the major constraints lie in the banking sector which makes the banks mostly responsible for impeding the successful inclusion of the RMG workers in the formal financial system. It should be noted that in available literature on business correspondent banking, which is a generic title for agent banking with perhaps more global applicability, there is evidence that the problems identified in this chapter are not unique to Bangladesh, particularly constraints related to support from the parent bank, incentives to agents, lack of appropriate products, and lack of financial literacy (Abrol, 2018; Handoo, 2010).

Discussion and recommendations

Considering the financial literacy of prospective clients as an essential driver of growth of the agent banking model, further emphasis should be given to this area in the future. As perceived by banks currently, the delivery of literacy programmes does not fall under the conventional banking activities. Therefore, it would be important to engage stakeholders such as the regulator so that financial literacy programmes are integrated into the agent banking model, since it is evident that they are integrally linked. For instance, in the interview with the NRBC Bank, it was recommended that the Bangladesh Bank mandate financial literacy as a CSR activity for banks with agent licences. The research on low-income customers in select cities in the US yields similar results (Servon & Kaestner, 2008) and underscores the importance of financial education of customers. Studies from India have highlighted the importance of financial literacy to business correspondent banking models (Abrol, 2018).

This study revealed that the banks would benefit from investing in training and deploying female customer relations officers when the target population is female RMG workers. The female customers were found to be comfortable with female agents or female customer relations officers only. They also tend to confide in female officers about household distress and are in the habit of saving with female officers in absolute trust that their husbands will not come to know about their savings. Female officers could also play an important role in refresher of knowledge and reinforcement of financial inclusion.

Shifting financial literacy to weekends at the community living areas for workers may be considered as it would also be effective for reeling in many other potential customers while prioritising their convenience. Alternative means of communicating financial literacy would be effective through audio visual material or through conventional behavioural change communication material such as flyers, posters, and leaflets. In addition, given the social context of Bangladesh, engagement of male family members, particularly husbands of married female workers, is imperative and financial literacy programmes need to engage them as well. There is evidence from available research on microfinance programmes that male family members play a key role in female decision making even when the female family members are the direct customers of financial institutions and, therefore, it is important to address male family members as well (Vonderlack-Navarro, 2010).

Another significant area is the suitable product development which can not only reflect RMG workers' lifestyles but also help to improve them. For instance, a Money Multiplier programme could be introduced to incentivise RMG workers to reach savings goals and earn higher interest. Alternatively, since RMG workers are also exposed to health hazards at workplaces, products could incentivise clients to save more by offering medical insurance if their average balance exceeds a pre-determined amount. More comprehensive research is necessary for achieving better understanding of the prerequisites of new banking product development in the future. Similar research has been undertaken that use innovative qualitative techniques such as the financial diaries approach to better understand customers' financial behaviour (McClatchey, 2013).

If agent banking outlets could serve as points from which workers receive their salaries, it would be easier to encourage workers to open salary accounts. For this reason, emphasis should be given in locating agent points close to bazaars or market places where the agents can service customers of different profiles. In addition, payroll processing would be important to be included in the agent banking product mix. Since RMG factories have come under media and civil society pressure to uphold higher standards of workers' rights, health, and safety, they have become suspicious towards external interference, particularly by development agencies. To overcome the obstacles regarding the factory personnel and to create sufficient incentives for senior management, it is envisaged that partnering with international RMG buyers who source garments products from the factories could be an important catalyst to scale-up.

Last but not the least; a widely accepted fact is that KYC (Know Your Customer) requirements are a deterrent to financial inclusion (Nkuna, Lapukeni, Kaude, & Kabango, 2018). Therefore, the banks could introduce more flexibility to RMG workers enabling them to open bank accounts more easily. For instance, banks could persuade the central bank to introduce tiered-KYC requirements where accounts with higher transactions and balances require successively higher forms of identification and documentation. In the long run, banks could leverage existing SIM registration or SMART card process to remove further identification requirements.

Conclusion

This study intended to underline the prevailing impediments both in the banking and non-banking sectors that are responsible for hampering the financial inclusion of the RMG workers in Bangladesh. Through this study it was found that a large portion of the existing obstacles exists in the banking sector itself. Although many commercial banks have initiated providing agent banking services for the deprived and marginalised sections of the society like the RMG workers, they are yet to realise the full potential of this field and act accordingly. There is deficiency of keenness among the banks in the case of treating agent banking as a major component of their functional structure and setting up individual divisions for its smooth operation.

This study also found that the banks need to further emphasise the proper branding of their agent banking products and educate their target customers about the advantages and profits of availing of this service. Carrying out frequent and effective financial literacy sessions for the target group at the time and place of their convenience is identified to be a feasible solution in this regard. In addition, hindering issues or persons like factory supervisors need to be educated in order to facilitate the workers in attending the sessions. This study also urges the emergence of taking proper steps to adequately incentivising the agents through increasing the number of services offered through them and also attract even more customers along the process. Concurrently, the agents need to be trained continuously in order to develop their capacity of handling more complicated transactions and other operations.

Another significant challenge highlighted in this study is the unnecessary complexity generated from the huge list of identification documents required for opening bank accounts. This process needs to be simplified while creating trust among the customers regarding the agents and their services. Apart from these, this study emphasises the substantial outcomes that can be brought forth through identifying and appointing more female agents and female financial counsellors to attract and sustain a bigger flow of female customers from the target group.

One of the primary limitations of this study was that it was concentrated on the two commercial banks considered for the project. Further research should be done with a larger number of commercial banks with agent banking provisions as sample for acquiring more generalisability of the findings. Existing constraints generated from the socio-economic conditions of the RMG workers should be studied to get the overall portrayal of the prevailing impediments of their financial inclusion in the context of Bangladesh.

Notes

1 The project 'Sarathi-Progress through Financial Inclusion' is aimed at bringing the female workforce of the Ready-Made Garments (RMG) industry of Bangladesh inside the sphere of formal financial services. The project has successfully finished its 19-month pilot phase funded by MetLife Foundation and Swiss Agency for Development. The goal of this project is to inspire and facilitate the RMG workers in gaining access to mainstream banks and commercial financial institutions. For reaching this goal the Sarathi project is supporting the creation of suitable financial products for the target group, developing alternative banking channels for easier access, and enhancing financial literacy among the target group while engaging them in financial transactions as account holders and clients.

2 Agent banking services are aimed at providing formal banking services to the unbanked. These services are provided by authorised agents of banks in agent points which are a lot smaller than the bank branches. These points are equipped with devices like point of sales (POS) devices, mobile phones, barcode scanners, computers, and biometric devices. Agent banking reduces the cost of setting up bank branches and thus allows the banks to extend their services to the marginalised population of the country (Khan & Woodard, 2016).

3 bKash is one of the most popular mobile financial services in Bangladesh. It runs as a subsidiary of BRAC Bank Limited, a private commercial bank in Bangladesh.

4 This study included two banks, Bank Asia and NRBC Bank, as the implementing partners of the pilot project. These two banks were considered for their willingness to do bottom-of-the-pyramid lending, readiness, and also market position vis-à-vis the banking sector.

5 Bank Asia: Bank Asia is a commercial bank in Bangladesh which was established in 1999.

6 NBRC Bank: NRB Commercial Bank Limited started its journey in Bangladesh from 2013. They are known for their migrants' sponsored banking system.

References

Abrol, V. (2018). Business correspondent model: a study of demand and supply. *Journal of Management, 5*(6), 1–12. ISSN Print: 2347–3940 and ISSN Online: 2347–3959.

Accenture and Care International. (2015). Within reach: how banks in emerging economies can grow profitably by being more inclusive. Care International and Accenture. Retrieved from https://insights.careinternational.org.uk/publications/within-reach-how-banks-in-emerging-economies-can-grow-profitably-by-being-more-inclusive

Aduda, J., & Kalunda, E. (2012). Financial inclusion and financial sector stability with reference to Kenya: a review of literature. *Journal of Applied Finance & Banking, 2*(6), 95–120. ISSN: 1792–6599 (online).

Afande, F. O., & Mbugua, S. W. (2015). Role of agent banking services in promotion of financial inclusion in Nyeri Town, Kenya. *Research Journal of Finance and Accounting, 6*(3), 148–174. ISSN: 2222–2847 (online).

Ainul, S., Hossain, M. I., Amin, S., & Rob, U. (2013). *Financial Inclusion of Female Garment Workers.* Dhaka: The Population Council, Inc. Retrieved from https://pdfs.semanticscholar.org/5efc/29cac27cd50d5ebcb87dc13e92493b08c5d3.pdf

Akter, S. (2016). Overview of financial inclusion in Bangladesh. *The Journal of the Study of Modern Society and Culture,* (63), 225–255. ISSN: 1345–8485.

Alo, J. N. (2019). Deposit through agent banking rises 122pc. Retrieved from *The Daily Star*: https://www.thedailystar.net/business/banking/news/deposit-through-agent-banking-rises-122pc-1701760

Amit, S. (2017). A closer look at financial inclusion in Bangladesh. *CES Thought Leadership* article. Retrieved from https://ces.ulab.edu.bd/wp-content/uploads/sites/18/2017/10/Financial-Inclusion-in-Bangladesh_v2_ULAB-CES_October-2017.pdf

Aro-Gordon, S. (2016). Effectiveness of financial inclusion strategy in Nigeria. *2nd International Conference on Inclusive Economic Growth and Sustainable Development,* (pp. 1–20). Mysuru, India: sdmimd.

Bangladesh Bank. (2013). *Regulations and Guidelines.* Retrieved from Bangladesh Bank: Central Bank of Bangladesh: https://www.bb.org.bd/aboutus/regulationguideline/psd/agentbanking_banks_v13.pdf

Berger, E., & Nakata, C. (2013). Implementing technologies for the financial services innovations in the base of the pyramid markets. *Journal of Product Innovation Management, 30*(6), 1199–1211. DOI: 10.1111/jpim.12054

Boateng, W. (2012). Evaluating the efficacy of focus group discussion (FGD) in qualitative social research. *International Journal of Business and Social Science, 3*(7), 54–57.

Braun, V. and Clarke, V. (2006). Using thematic analysis in psychology. *Qualitative Research in Psychology, 3*(2), 77–101. ISSN 1478–0887.

Bryman, A., & Burgess, R. G. (1994). *Analyzing Qualitative Data.* London: Routledge. ISBN: 0–203–41308–3.

CARE Bangladesh. (2017). *Situation Analysis on Financial Inclusion for Female RMG Workers.* Dhaka: CARE Bangladesh. Retrieved from http://www.carebangladesh.org/publication/Publication_8660144.pdf

Damodaran, A. (2012). Financial inclusion: issues and challenges. *AKGEC International Journal of Technology, 4*(2), 54–59.

Dawson, S., Manderson, L., & Tallo, V. L. (1993). *A Manual for the Use of Focus Groups.* Boston, USA: International Nutrition Foundation for Developing Countries (INFDC). ISBN: 0–9635522-2–8.

Demirgüç-Kunt, A., Klapper, L., Singer, D., Ansar, S., & Hess, J. (2017). *The Global Findex Database 2017: Measuring Financial Inclusion and the Fintech Revolution*. Washington DC: The World Bank. DOI: 10.1596/978-1-4648-1259-0.

Dey, I. (1993). *Qualitative Data Analysis: A User-friendly Guide for Social Scientist*. London: Routledge. ISBN: 0–203–72073-3.

Dutch-Bangla Bank. (n.d.). *Dutch-Bangla Bank Agent Banking*. Retrieved from Dutch-Bangla Bank Limited: https://www.dutchbanglabank.com/agent-banking/agent banking.html

Gaisina, S., & Kaidarova, L. (2017). Financial literacy of rural population as a determinant of saving behavior in Kazakhstan. *Rural Sustainability Research, 38*(333), 32–42. ISSN: 2256–0939.

Hammond, A. L., Kramer, W. J., Katz, R. S., Tran, J. T., & Walker, C. (2007). *The Next 4 Billion: Market Size and Business Strategy at the Base of the Pyramid*. Washington DC: World Resource Institute and International Finance Corporation. ISBN: 1–56973-625-1.

Handoo, J. (2010). Financial inclusion in India: integration, policy and market at bottom of the pyramid. *SSRN Electronic Journal*, 1–13. DOI: 10.2139/ssrn.1628564.

Ho, J. (2017). Why agent banking is a win-win. Retrieved from *Business Today*: https://www.businesstoday.in/opinion/columns/why-agent-banking-is-a-win-win/story/258171.html

Hossain, M., Dey, E. K., & Afzal, M. H. (2015). *Sustainable Implementation of Agent Banking Management in Rural Areas of Bangladesh to Evade Financial Fragility among Unbanked People*. Dhaka, Bangladesh. Retrieved from http://www.iit.du.ac.bd/about_iit/download/133

ICT Division. (2015). *Digital ID for Digital Bangladesh*. Dhaka: ICT Division, Ministry of Posts, Telecommunication and Information Technology.

Islam, S. (2018). The rapid growth of agent banking in Bangladesh. Retrieved from *Dhaka Tribune*: https://www.dhakatribune.com/business/2018/06/03/the-rapid-growth-of-agent-banking-in-bangladesh

Khan, A. R., & Woodard, J. (2016). *Tipsheet: Agent Banking 101*. Dhaka: USAID. Retrieved from https://www.marketlinks.org/sites/marketlinks.org/files/resource/files/Tipsheet_AgentBanking101_July2016.pdf

Kolk, A., Rivera-Santos, M., & Rufin, C. (2014). reviewing a decade of research on the 'base/bottom of the pyramid' (BOP) concept. *Business and Society, 53*(3), 338–477. DOI: 10.1177/0007650312474928.

Lehman, J. (2010). *Operational Challenges of Agent Banking Systems*. Bill & Melinda Gates Foundation. Retrieved from https://docs.gatesfoundation.org/documents/operational-challenges.pdf

Lotto, J. (2016). The role of agency banking in promoting financial inclusion: descriptive analytical evidence from Tanzania. *European Journal of Business and Management, 8*(22), 231–240. ISSN: 2222–2389 (online).

Mas, I., & Siedek, H. (2008). *Banking through Networks of Retail Agents*. Washington DC: CGAP. Retrieved from http://documents.worldbank.org/curated/en/374441468330976181/pdf/445880NWP0BOX31gents0FN14701PUBLIC1.pdf

McClatchey, M. (2013). *An Impact Evaluation of BRAC's Microfinance Program in Uganda*. BRAC Uganda. Retrieved from https://pdfs.semanticscholar.org/c603/f424e75528f963e42b6d432052792aa7a6c7.pdf

Mishra, L. (2016). Focus group discussion in qualitative research. *Techno Learn, 6*(1), 1–5. Retrieved from http://ndpublisher.in/admin/issues/tlV6N1a.pdf

Mwende, M. J., Bichanga, J., & Mosoti, J. (2015). Investigation on importance of agency banking in provision of banking services in Kenya: (a case of equity bank) in Kitui Central District, Kitui County, Kenya. *International Journal of Scientific and Research Publications, 5*(10), 1–13. ISSN: 2250–3153.

Ndegwa, P. M. (2017). An analysis of the effectiveness of agency banking as a financial inclusion strategy in commercial banks (a survey of selected commercial banks in Kiambu Town). *International Journal of Business and Management Invention, 6*(8), 67–75. ISSN: 2319–8028 (online).

Nkuna, O., Lapukeni, A. F., Kaude, P., & Kabango, G. (2018). The role of commercial banks on financial inclusion in Malawi. *Open Journal of Business and Management*, 812–832. DOI: 10.4236/ojbm.2018.64061.

Parvez, J., Islam, A., & Woodard, J. (2015). *Mobile Financial Services in Bangladesh: A Survey of Current Services, Regulations, and Usage in Select USAID Projects.* Dhaka: USAID. ISBN: 0–89492–920–8.

Rahman, B. (2016). The impact of agency banking to the development of SME sector: the case of Bangladesh. *World Journal of Social Sciences, 6*(3), 59–75. Retrieved from http://www.wjsspapers.com/static/documents/September/2016/5.%20Benazir.pdf

Santu, T. C., Mawanza, W., & Muredzi, V. (2017). An evaluation of the agency banking model adopted by Zimbabwean commercial banks. *Journal of Finance and Bank Management, 5*(2), 58–66. DOI: 10.15640/jfbm.v5n2a6.

Selvarajan, S. K. (2018). Financial inclusion: at the bottom of the pyramid. *Institutions and Economies*, pp. 129–131. ISSN: 2232-1349.

Servon, L. J., & Kaestner, R. (2008). Consumer financial literacy and the impact of online banking on the financial behavior of lower-income bank customers. *The Journal of Consumer Affairs, 42*(2), 271–305. ISSN: 0022–0078.

Tasavori, M., Ghauri, P., & Zaefarian. (2014). The entry of multinational companies to the base of the pyramid: a network perspective. In Y. Temouri, & J. C., *International Business and Institutions after the Financial Crisis.* London: The Academy of International Business. ISBN Print: 978-1-349–47443-1 and ISBN Online: 978-1-137–36720-4.

Thakur, A., Sahoo, S., Barooah, P., Sivalingam, I., & Njoroge, G. (2016). *Agency Banking: How Female Agents Make a Difference.* Retrieved from Microsave: http://blog.microsave.net/2016/04/05/agency-banking-how-female-agents-make-a-difference/

The Daily Star. (April 9, 2018). Agent banking most useful for financial inclusion: analysts. Retrieved from *The Daily Star*: https://www.thedailystar.net/business/banking/agent-banking-most-useful-financial-inclusion-analysts-1560013

The World Bank. (n.d.). *Financial Inclusion Overview.* Retrieved from The World Bank: https://www.worldbank.org/en/topic/financialinclusion/overview

Thomas, D. R. (2006). A general inductive approach for analyzing qualitative evaluation data. *American Journal of Evaluation, 27*(2), 237–246. DOI: https://doi.org/10.1177/1098214005283748.

TP, S. M. (2014). Awareness and access of financial inclusion drive: a study of below poverty line households in Kerala. *Global Journal of Commerce & Management* Perspective, 3(4), 201–214. ISSN: 2319–7285.

Vonderlack-Navarro, R. (2010). Targeting women versus addressing gender in microcredit: lessons from Honduras. *Affilia: Journal of Women and Social Work, 25*(2), 123–134. DOI: 10.1177/0886109910364356.

Appendix

Pre-determined theme	Excerpts	Sub-themes	Codes
Financial literacy programmes (FLP)	We could not learn much from the financial literacy sessions	Poor learning	FLP1
	Financial counsellors are not clearly incentivised	Not incentivised	FLP2
	The floor manager doesn't permit us to attend the sessions	Floor manager	FLP3
	The workers tend to take naps or pray during lunch break rather than attending the sessions	Timing of sessions	FLP4
	There is no enough number of staffs in banks to deploy in agent banking area	Lack of stuff	FLP5
Product development (PD)	Product approval takes up a lot of time	Time consuming	PD1
	A lot of documents are required to commence with developing a new product	Excessive documents	PD2
Agent banking set-up and roll-out (ABSR)	Agents cannot profit enough only by offering savings and DPs products	Insufficient profit	ABSR1
	The female workers do not feel comfortable around male agents	Gender of agent	ABSR2
	There are only a few female agents in the banks	Few female agents	ABSR3
	The banks gave less than adequate efforts in promoting agent banking	Inadequate promotion	ABSR4
	The agents did not receive enough training	Insufficient training	ABSR5
Bank account opening and usage (BAOU)	NRBC takes up to 5 days to activate an account	Delayed activation	BAOU1
	Some of the workers do not trust the agents	Lack of trust	BAOU2
	They ask for a lot of documents and NID for opening a bank account	NID possession	BAOU3

6 Contribution and efficiency of social businesses in poverty reduction in Iran

Mina Mohammadi Khorasani

Introduction

After the World Summit on Sustainable Development, where governments, NGOs (non- governmental organization), businesses, and other influential agents gathered, and poverty came into consideration as a major global challenge that requires their serious and simultaneous contribution, Base of the Pyramid (BOP) attracted much attention. It was accepted as a serious academic discourse and soon became prevalent in the management literature and practice of large companies. In the BOP argument, the world's poor are known as a 'Bottom of the Pyramid' population and a market-based approach is suggested for poverty alleviation (Prahalad & Hammond, 2002; Prahalad, 2002). Prahalad (2009) brings up the concept and persuades MNCs (multinational companies) to enter this so-called *large untapped market* with an emphasis on innovation in products and services providing to the poor communities to help poverty alleviation while maintaining and increasing their profits (Prahalad, 2009).

BOP has undergone lots of ups and downs during the last seventeen years: from BOP 1.0 which was mainly focused on the sales to the poor societies, to BOP 2.0 as a result of management, economic, and even ethical criticisms (Karnani, 2006). This led to a concept of co-creation and engagement of the poor in the production chain and encouraging them towards entrepreneurship (Simanis & Hart, 2008). Nevertheless, studies on the initiatives and practices of large companies show that the BOP approach has failed to fulfil its basic promises about companies' profit making and poverty alleviation (Garrette, & Karnani, 2010). In some cases, these initiatives/projects have either transformed into NGOs and corporate social responsibilities or even shifted their target society towards the middle-class population to survive. Such approaches have sometimes made situations even worse for the societies they intended to serve (Agnihotri, 2012; Crabtree, 2007).

Since BOP is a market-based approach, its suggested strategy for poverty alleviation goes through merging the communities of the 'world's poor' into the global market (Peredo, Montgomery, & McLean, 2018). Besides the criticism on the BOP approach in practice, which led to its evolution, some have addressed the whole strategy, criticising the absolute top-down involvement of private companies in socio-economic development for the poor. Bonsu and Polsa (2011) argue that BOP is a neoliberal project aimed at solving the problem of shrinking markets of MNCs (Bonsu & Polsa, 2011). Peredo et al. (2018) argue that, regardless of all its claims for innovation, BOP is nothing but a new declaration of the so-called – yet widely censored – theory of modernisation. Emphasising the fact that, in many academic environments, BOP is virtually substituted for the word poverty, they conclude that BOP aims to enhance the imperialism hegemony and to eliminate any other form of economic alternatives for poverty alleviation (Peredo et al., 2018).

Considering the general inefficient image of BOP 1.0 and BOP 2.0 which mainly highlights the role of an external agent (mostly large multinational companies) to reduce poverty, in recent years efforts have been made to move towards BOP 3.0 as a more inclusive and sustainable strategy (Dasgupta & Hart, 2017). In the BOP 3.0 model, development is not defined solely by income generation and economic growth; it is instead a transformation and structural change. This new model requires more efforts to explore surrounding issues associated with poverty as well as to find roots and causes. That is, BOP 3.0 is an inside-outward strategy to establish a precise understanding of the local aspects of poverty and adopt community-based strategies to build self-reliant and coherent societies to underpin market-based initiatives (Chmielewski, Dembek, & Beckett, 2018). Everywhere in the world, poverty has its specific properties. Poverty is not a mere economic phenomenon; it has different social, political, cultural, and environmental attributes. This way, BOP 3.0 is similar to the social business concept. It is worth mentioning that, having more or less floating meanings with no fixed frameworks, both concepts are still developing. In this study it is noted that:

- based on its fundamental definition, every BOP model requires the presence of an external agent of change (multinational companies and/or non-local agents); and it is also promised that the agents will make profit this way (Dembek, Sivasubramaniam, & Chmielewski, 2019; London, 2007).
- same as other forms of business, social businesses also seek profits, although these are not limited to economic and financial interests only. Instead, creating positive social impacts is defined as a part of their profit and even their main mission (Borzaga, Galera, & Nogales, 2008; Yunus, Moingeon, & Lehmann-Ortega, 2010).
- these positive impacts address a wide range of contexts such as women's and children's rights, environmental issues, and poverty. It is also noted that sometimes social businesses take the form of NGOs which are dependent on grants and donations for survival. Yet, there are other organizations that work in a sustainable way quite independently from external financial aids. Such enterprises could be defined as BOP 3.0 approaches in which the main focus is transformed from economy towards the community.

In one of the very few BOP articles published about Iran, Jazani and Khat-avakhotan (2011) estimated the population of Iranian BOP in 2008 as 25,920,000 people based on a combined model of income and inflation rate (Jazani & Khatavakhotan, 2011). With refer to the reports of Statistical Centre of Iran and the 70 million population of Iran in the same year, this is equivalent to 37% of the country's population, whereas, according to official data and experts' remarks (Madani, 2018), the poverty ratio has been drastically increased over years which corresponds to the Gini coefficient data of the Central Bank of Iran (Tsd.cbi.ir, 2019), indicating increased inequality and class discrimination. Yet, a serious context has not formed to activate BOP discourse in Iran. It is presumably because of the special international situation of Iran throughout these 17 years of BOP history in academic and management discussions, and due to the limitations that are imposed on the country's international economic interactions in several periods of time. That is, despite widespread poverty in the country and the strict implementation of structural adjustment policies, the Iranian economy has practically lost access to international markets (Garshasbi & Yusefi, 2016). Consequently, according to the nature of BOP 1.0 and BOP 2.0 that mainly emphasises the contribution of large corporations from developed economics (Dasgupta & Hart, 2017), experts were reluctant to develop and study these approaches in Iran. However, since BOP 3.0 is more focused on local roots of poverty pursuing a community-based strategy, it seems that even despite international limitations, there is a gap for BOP 3.0 research and literature to investigate special features of poverty and poverty alleviation solutions in Iran within the framework of this approach.

Methodology

This is a qualitative interview study, focused on the case of Iran. After providing brief statistical data about poverty spread in Iran with reference to the official channels such as Parliament Research Centre of Iran and Central Bank of Iran; the main part of this study deals with experts' opinions through direct interviews and/or referring to their comments and statements elsewhere.

Academia experts were directly interviewed to talk about topics of 'roots of poverty spread in Iran' and 'the role of civil society in poverty reduction'; namely:

Hassan Taee; Head of Economy Group and Associate Professor of Economics Management and Development at Allameh Tabataba'i University in Tehran; Former Deputy Minister of Cooperatives, Labour Social Welfare. Direct interview at Allameh Tabataba'i University; dated December 5, 2018; Duration: 60 min.

Hossein Raghfar; Associate Professor of Economics and Director of the Institute for Economic and Social Studies at Alzahra University, Tehran. Direct interview; Alzahra University; dated November 24, 2018; Duration 60 min.

Reza Omidi; Assistant Professor of Social Sciences at University of Tehran, Tehran. Direct interview; University of Tehran; dated December 1 2018; Duration: 20 min.

In order to provide a more comprehensive image, opinions of other experts were also observed. Such data were collected from their speeches in academic environments (with reference to relative media reports and recorded audios); namely:

Ahmad Meidari; PhD in Economics, University of Tehran, Deputy Minister of Cooperatives, Labour Social Welfare. Data collection source: 'Poverty trap: In search of the way out' Scientific conference; held at University of Tehran; dated October 28, 2018 (recorded audio and media reports of the conference).

Sara Mazinani Shariati; Assistant Professor of Social Sciences at University of Tehran, Tehran. Data collection source: 'Poverty trap: In search of the way out' Scientific conference; held at University of Tehran; dated October 28, 2018 (recorded audio and media reports of the conference).

Saeed Madani Qahfarokhi; PhD in Criminology, University of Social Welfare & Rehabilitation Sciences, Tehran. Data collection source: 'Poverty trap: In search of the way out' Scientific conference; held at University of Tehran; dated October 28, 2018 (recorded audio and media reports of the conference).

By putting together the views of experts, a descriptive picture of poverty in Iran is presented exploring its political, social, economic, and cultural aspects.

Social business is suggested as a territory for civil society to play a role in improving the livelihood of certain groups of society within the frameworks and principals of BOP 3.0 strategy. For this purpose, cofounders/directors of several social business organizations were invited to explain their targets, priorities, strategies, failures, successes, challenges, and hopes throughout their mission. Having the priority of covering different legal forms of such organizations, and due to their availability and desire to response, finally three organizations that are active in three frameworks of private owned enterprise, NGO, and start-up were interviewed; namely:

Narges Tayebat; Co-founder of Mehrbaf (Private owned enterprise). Direct interview at Mehrbaf office dated November 24, 2018, duration 60 min; plus email correspondences November 25 – November 30, 2018.

Faezeh Derakhshani; Co-founder of Dastadast (NGO). Direct interview through email correspondences November 6–10, 2018.

Mohammad Ghaempanah; Co-founder of Keshmoon (Startup). Direct interview (on phone) December 22, 2018, duration 70 min.

Interviews started with an introduction about the scope of this study and the addressed parties answered questions about: nature of the business, targeted social impact, registered form of business, their commitment to the targeted social impact, sustainability of their business, innovations, legal constraints or challenges, contribution of international organizations in their business improvement, and finally their future perspectives.

With reference to the overall image of poverty, its roots, and characteristics in Iran that is derived from the experts' opinions section and the real experiences of interviewed social business owners, the contribution of social business in poverty reduction is discussed.

What does official data say?

In December 2018, Parliament Research Centre of Iran published two reports about the poverty spread in Iran and poverty distribution in different areas of the country during 1395[1] and 1397.[2] Despite the importance of identification of poor groups, it was after almost a decade that official assessments of poverty line were publicly released in 2018. The calculations of both reports are based on absolute poverty that is 'the inability to attain the minimum standard of living' and the food poverty line of at least 2100 calories per day (Shahbazian, Abdollahi, Einian, & Kaviani, 2018a; Shahbazian, Abdollahi, Einian, & Kaviani 2018b). Since there is a variety of regional lifestyles and price index levels in Iran, instead of a single countrywide poverty line, the poverty lines of different urban and rural areas were calculated for different regions. In 1395,[3] almost 15% of the total urban population and 12% of the total rural population were living below the absolute poverty line; around 65% of the rural households and 30–40% urban population of three poorest provinces suffered from food poverty (Shahbazian et al., 2018b).

While the absolute poverty line has increased by 24% from summer 2017 to summer 2018, the Parliament Research Centre predicts an imminent increase in the population of absolute poor and offers a series of recommendations for the implementation of supportive policies.

UN Human Rights defines poverty as a multidimensional phenomenon that encompasses a lack of both income and the basic capabilities to live in dignity (Office of the High Commissioner for Human Rights, 2012). This includes a wide range of depravations of human and social rights, rather than a mere economic problem. Poverty assessment models that compare incomes with the poverty line are not explicit. The connection of income and capabilities significantly depends on several factors such as age, gender, geographic location, environment, diseases, and any other factor that is out of their control (Raghfar, Babapour, & Yazdanpanah, 2016).

Several organizations including the State Welfare Organization, Imam Khomeini Relief Foundation, Astan Quds Razavi, Organization of Targeted Subsidies, and many others aim to fight poverty in Iran. Yet, the result of their forty years of activities in a country with massive shares of global oil and gas resources shows high degrees of inequality and poverty, and there is no sign of an inclusive poverty alleviation approach. Despite the fact that all five-year governmental development plans include some poverty alleviation policies, they have not resulted in an effective reduction in poverty (Raghfar et al., 2016).

Origins of poverty in Iran

Many evidences suggest that poverty and inequality are stable, resilient, and steady in Iran. Referring to the Central Bank reports of Gini coefficient which has stayed around 0.37–0.40 during all forty years of post-revolution, Madani (2018) concludes that the attempts to reduce inequality have always faced resilience. Inequality has risen and at present the ratio of the expenditure share of the wealthy 10 per cent is 14 times larger than the share of the poor. Poverty is reproduced and constantly imposed on the society through existing structures. In this way, he classifies the causes of status quo on poverty and inequality into four groups (Madani, 2018).

First of all, non-comprehensive poverty alleviation programmes failed to observe the structures and instead of fighting poverty, efforts were focused on dealing with the poor. In that sense, these programmes were effect-oriented and not structural. Secondly, the institutional structures were conflicting. In post-revolution Iran, in addition to the public and private sectors, a third public non-governmental sector was recognised which initially included ten organizations. According to Madani (2018), the main problem is that these major organizations were practically working unmonitored, almost outside the control of the Supreme Audit Court of Iran and authority of the State. While benefiting from a special political power, they gradually became very large economic powers and later new similar organizations emerged. These institutions nowadays form large economic and financial holdings that mostly work under no independent external surveillance and the profits of their activities are distributed among specific groups of society. Third of all, there is a problematic circuit of capital in Iran. When such institutions with huge financial resources and political power enter the market, they attempt to earn more profit and their orientation shifts to financial goals instead of industrial and productive activities. This circuit of capital in the financial sector exacerbates inequality and, consequently, poverty in Iran. Fourthly, as a result of mismanagement of oil revenues, there is a structural inflation (Madani, 2018).

The costs and benefits of many today's decisions will show up in the next generations. That's why intergenerational challenges and time-bound decisions should be observed as root causes of poverty. Water resources management is an obvious example of wrong time-bound policies in Iran which brought a temporary satisfaction among special groups of farmers who got free and unlimited access to water at a certain period of time; but now, the country is facing a great environmental crisis. Almost all provinces encounter water crisis in different forms namely loss of underground water recourses or drying wetlands and lakes (Meidari, 2018). Meidari (2018) believes that political economy and reforms from top-down are the right path to confront the problem. If poverty is a product of dominance of interests, a new model is required to change the power distribution in Iran (Meidari, 2018). Otherwise, all efforts will be limited to lower levels that result in some temporary easing effects only. Raghfar[4] (2018) also believes that poverty is a product of the socio-political system. According to Raghfar (2018), inequality is the root cause of poverty all over the world and in the case of Iran, the neoliberal policies of economic decision makers over the past three decades are responsible for the spread and reproduction of inequalities. Raghfar (2018) believes that these policies, derived from post-war economic adjustment programmes that were implemented under the name of privatisation, resulted in an extreme individualism that dominated the society and destroyed many social values. Raghfar (2018) continues to take Japan as an example of a poor country in terms of natural resources compared with Iran. In Japan, the social policies with a focus on 'employment for all' boost the economy (Raghfar, 2018).

This leads to another important cause of poverty in Iran, which is unemployment. A survey from Iran's Statistics Centre (2017) shows that in 1396,[5] 12.6% of active labour resources were unemployed. The highest share of employment is within the service sector with a rate of 49.8%. Industry and agriculture sectors are attributed to 31.5% and 18.7% of the total employed population respectively (Iran's Statistics Centre, 2017). However, alongside the very narrow standard definition of unemployment — which is the basis for the Statistical Centre of Iran reports — a broader definition stands for decent work. Income earner of the country's poorest households (first to third income/expenditure deciles) is whether a woman or an informal worker or does not have a permanent job (Taee, 2018). It implies that the situation of the labour market and its fluctuations directly and significantly affects the subsistence and livelihood of the poorest groups. Many people work few hours a week and many may work over 40 hours a week but remain below the poverty line. So, the reported 12.6% (3 million) unemployed population refers to the worst situation of not having a job for even one hour per week.

From Iran's Constitution the concept of 'full employment' is inferred as the government's responsibility. Article 28 of the Constitution specifically assigns this duty to the government 'to provide every citizen with the opportunity to work and to create equal conditions for obtaining it'. Given that human dignity is in the core of Iran's Constitution (Chapter 3; The rights of the people, articles 19 to 42, I.R.I. Const., 1989), and the fact that people's job has a great influence on their social identity, Raghfar (2018) expects the focus of the public policies to be on 'decent work' and 'fair wage' for all. This is observed in article 43 of Iran's Constitution - the country's economy system is based on several key criteria including '[e]nsuring conditions and opportunities of employment for everyone, with a view to attaining full employment'. However, referring to the tax structures and the banking facilities that are mainly allocated to the trading sector, Raghfar (2018) concludes that production is a very costly activity in Iran and the manufacturing sector that is capable of creating jobs and added value is heavily in trouble. That is why capital runs away from the manufacturing sector and instead, non-productive businesses are expanding (Raghfar, 2018).

A report of the 500 top Iranian companies indicates that 57% of the assets and 25.5% of the 100 best-seller Iranian companies belong to the banks and credit institutions (Industrial Management Institute, 2017). These figures indicate that the main feature of Iran's economy is financialisation, and its unproductive, non-labour intensive character (Madani, 2018).

Khavand (2018) assumes that the Iranian economy has lost its potential for entrepreneurship thus lagging behind global development and this explains the spread of poverty in the country. The right way to deal with poverty is to create jobs, and establishing manufacturing firms to create employment opportunities requires investment. Investment, both domestic and foreign, needs a climate of trust and in its absence. According to Khavand (2018), Iran is not able to achieve the necessary productive capacity for employment resulting in millions of citizens living in absolute poverty.

The role of civil society: organizing, networking, empowering

If encountering poverty and inequality is in the debate of political power, then as long as the relation of political power to the society and its functions in the creation of structural inequalities are not settled in the right way, a meaningful confrontation with poverty will not be possible.

Shariati[6] (2018) enters the debate from the standpoint of a sociologist. Since political power is responsible for poverty alleviation and also at present accused of poverty reproduction, she advocates for civic activities. She acknowledges the fact that civic activities won't completely eradicate poverty states that organizing a strong civil society is the only path towards liberation. Emphasising the role of science production, the creation of a model movement, and the solidarity between the poor, Shariati (2018) presents the model of *Knowledge against Poverty* research chairs to justify her point of view. She continues by saying that knowledge of various fields of economics, sociology, psychology, statistics, etc. is accumulated over time and the task of such research chairs is to formulate and share this accumulated knowledge of poverty and build up methodology. This will equip the field activists in their fight with poverty. According to her, an important functionality of a community-based approach is to induce the sensibility of students and scholars so that they expand their research on it and a new epistemology in the field of poverty alleviation will be generated. It is the social responsibility of experts to facilitate the growth and networking of civic organizations, raising the voices of deprived and silent groups in different ways, and persisting in the human rights on the basis of country's existing laws. The capacity of social media is significant here (Shariati, 2018).

According to Taee[7] (2018), any social activity of university scholars that leads to empowerment of human beings is a root of social changes. Observing a major gap in empowering and educating capable and creative individuals who can advance a social project or organize a social event, for about 10 years he has been conducting educational courses and workshops in the most deprived areas in Sistan and Balouchestan province to encourage reliance on talents and self-confidence. The workshops audience include different groups of students, teachers, rural mayors, and young university graduates. Many infrastructural problems remain out of the control of mayors and local authorities. Yet, because most of the population lives in rural areas, rural mayors play an important role in these communities. Therefore, local empowerment and rural development workshops are held with an emphasis on increasing social participation with the contribution of three pillars of rural mayors (government), local communities, and NGOs. Mayors learn to draft and prepare business plans to later be connected to governmental funds such as the Omid Entrepreneurship Fund or Rural Development Fund to support small and rural businesses and receive facilities. *Idea-raising* and from *idea to business workshops* are also held for university graduates to educate and empower them for starting productive economic activities. They normally start with home-based businesses and may turn to formal microenterprises or move toward SMEs (small and medium sized enterprises) in the next stages. A positive overall business environment is however a key for the continuity of the empowerment, entrepreneurship, and sustainability (Taee, 2018).

People voluntarily contribute in these events as their social responsibility and the aim is to promote a culture of self-reliant community building and growing. These are supported by the province's Science and Technology Park, Omid Entrepreneurship Fund, and other governmental organizations.

Meidari (2018) believes that the governments should not be left carefree of the fight against poverty. The Iranian governments have huge oil revenues that belong to all Iranians and must be dedicated to poverty eradication. In his terms, there may be disagreements over the poverty alleviation strategies, but there should not be any disagreement over the necessity of the resources allocation to solve this problem on which the question rises where and for what purpose the oil revenues will be spent if they are not meant for social justice and poverty alleviation (Meidari, 2018).

This point of view finds the current macroeconomic policies of the country guilty for producing inequality and poverty, and, while appreciating the efforts of civil society in making positive impacts, correctly warns that it would be unrealistic if we focus on micro-level approaches and put the burden on the part of individuals. It would be dangerous too as it lets the government off the hook (Omidi, 2018).

Contribution of social businesses in a positive civic approach

A proposal for the participation of civic activists is the expansion of a social business idea aimed at reducing the sufferings of the population involved in poverty. As discussed, many experts are addressing the sphere of governance and macroeconomic management to deal with poverty. And yet, it is not the viewpoint of local experts only. Muhammad Yunus[8] – in an interview on the efficiency of social business and microfinance in Iran – sets out the same concerns. According to him, the idea of launching Grameen Bank and providing microfinance to the poor was initially planned for very poor countries like Bangladesh. He doubts if such a model is really needed or would work well in a rich country like Iran. In other words, if the oil resources are managed and spent in a proper way, why are there still poor people in Iran (Khoshbin, 2013).

Poverty is a serious condition of necessity that has the potential of developing community-based movements. Condition of necessity, as observed by Defourny and Develtere (2009), is the economic or socio-economic condition that still prevails in the world and encourages social economy. Social economy has showed up in different forms such as cooperatives, foundations, and associations with a history that backs to the oldest forms of human associations (Defourny & Develtere, 2009).

The term *social business* was introduced in the 1990s to seek social improvement alongside the economic ambitions. It intends to highlight and promote entrepreneurial activities focused on social aims and does not seek to replace existing concepts for the third sector such as the social economy or the non-profit sector. Social businesses contribute to work towards integration thus assisting in the development of disadvantaged areas (Borzaga, Galera, & Nogales, 2008). Since the emergence of the term, it has been practised in different legal forms and structures. When there is no legal definition for such a debatable concept, there are always chances for misuse or wrong interpretation. A recent case is the publication of a highly criticised advertisement in late 2018 that was inviting people to come up with their innovative job creation ideas for children. The advertisement was published by the National Social Innovation Centre and was very frankly talking about the high potential of children to work, while having very low expectation when it comes to the working conditions and wages, and that it is 'the best opportunity for job creation' (Shargh Daily, 2018). Although, the advertisement faced serious criticism from different groups of social activists and the publisher removed it from their website, it should be noted that this has been an outcome of a governmental sponsored, university-based national research centre. This is an example of what Cieslik (2018) refers to as social entrepreneurship as mitigation and its adaptability with neoliberal systems. She classifies the social enterprise literature in two mainstreams of mitigation and transformation that are products of two different political approaches. According to her, the core assumption of the currently hegemonic social enterprise as mitigation discourse is that they match the existing neoliberal system and are able to make social impact while making profit in the existing dominated political structure. On the other hand, the discourse of social entrepreneurship as transformation argues that the social enterprise concept is deeply political as bringing sustainable social impact is not only about providing the missing services to the deprived people, but also targeting the political structures that reproduce the problems. Transformation discourse pursues a system of increased social justice and more equitable distribution of resources. In this sense, it emphasises the role of the civil society while considering the initiatives that provide effective and sustainable solutions to make social impact (Cieslik, 2018). It is in the same way that Omidi (2018) warns about the depoliticisation of poverty and that, in the literature of social business, there is a serious potential to attribute the whole problem to the individuals and pull the structure aside (Omidi, 2018).

In Iran, many NGOs, university volunteer teams, businesses, and charities are dealing with poverty without relying on governmental aids. Some of these work under the name of social business, others are targeting social problems without holding a specific label. In order to evaluate the effectiveness and mechanism of social businesses contribution in poverty alleviation, organizations with different approaches and social aims were contacted for interviews. Due to the non-availability and lack of response from some, finally the founders of three organizations (Mehrbaf, Dastadast, Keshmoon) were interviewed with questions about the nature of business, extent of their social impact, legal constraints, and their contribution to poverty reduction. They offered suggestions to improve the situation as well. In order to see which legal structure can better serve the goal of poverty alleviation and match BOP 3.0 discourse, attention was paid to their three different structures as well. Mehrbaf works as a for- profit private enterprise, Dastadast is a NGO, and Keshmoon is a startup trying to shift to the 'knowledge enterprise' framework.

Mehrbaf

The idea of Mehrbaf entrepreneurship project was formed in January 2012. The founders are three women with a background of women and children related social activities in NGOs since the 1990s. Having such theoretical and practical background, in 2011 they decided to start an entrepreneurship business to empower women by creating jobs for them. The business plan was prepared around the core idea that having an independent job, fair wage, and economic identity is a necessity for women. The plan covers three stages of short, medium, and long-term targets while skill training remains as its fundamental basis in all three phases (Tayebat, 2018).

Mehrbaf is a knitwear producing workshop. According to Narges Tayebat (2018) – one of the cofounders – they wanted the business to comply with the basic characteristics of an entrepreneurship such as creativity, development, and reviving the native arts and techniques while having an eye towards the history of Iranians being skilful in hand weaving, knitting, and dyeing of clothes, carpets, and rugs. The originality, design, and colouring of the textiles that come from various regions of Iran are unique and well known all over the world. Furthermore, during the war in the 1980s and sanction periods, Iranian home-staying women, especially in Tehran and its neighbouring towns, bought knitting machines and produced clothes for their family and relatives. So, these women already knew how to work with knitting machines (Tayebat, 2018).

Targeted social impact: women empowerment and creating sustainable job opportunities for them

The founders of Mehrbaf intended to design a workshop model for women's employment so that they take part in training courses, benefit from having an economic identity, and work in a secure environment where their dignity is well observed and offers them the flexibility to adopt with their special social requirements. All employees receive a regular monthly salary in accordance with Iranian labour law, and benefit from social insurances that give them the opportunity to improve their and their family's education, health, and economic security. The main goal of Mehrbaf is the creation of jobs for women. Women's financial independence improves the life quality of family and their children's access to higher education (Tayebat, 2018)

Nature and registered framework of business

Mehrbaf is a production enterprise that is registered as a private company, works according to the regulations of for-profit companies, and their paid taxes are equal to the taxes determined for for-profit companies. The nature of business, however, is a social business model.

Mehrbaf is legally classified as a home-based business – though they do not work at home. The cofounders insist on bringing women out of their homes and gathering them in a real formal working environment to promote their social engagement and prestige. As Tayebat (2018) states, the entrepreneurship office of the Ministry of Cooperatives, Labour, and Social Welfare still has no definite criterions for entrepreneurship and is far away from instating a special legal structure for registration of social businesses (Tayebat, 2018).

Commitment to the targeted social impact

As clearly mentioned in their business plan, the founders are committed to the principle of spending any gained profit on the development and expansion of the workshop to create more job opportunities for women. That's why the founders do not take any profit but receive a certain monthly salary like the employees. At the end of each year, the managers hold a meeting with colleagues and discuss problems and achievements of all co-workers, the financial situation, and the procedure of work. Several principles are observed in Mehrbaf which according to Tyaebat distinguish their business from regular for-profit companies:

- All the employees of Mehrbaf can benefit from free skill training courses.
- Due to the difficulties that small enterprises face in the current business environment and general economic situation of Iran, many do not commit to pay for the employees' social insurance or even their regular monthly salaries. Mehrbaf always pays its employer share for employees' insurance, the least salary is based on what is determined by Iranian labour law, and those with more working experience receive higher amounts.
- The employees of Mehrbaf work for 186 hours per month which is less than the working hours determined by the Ministry of Labour.
- Mothers of young children are allowed to have flexible working hours. They also have the option to work at home in exchange for their occasional absence from work.
- All designed tasks are first evaluated by a consulting team of young university graduates in arts and fashion, then briefly tested in the market, and finally introduced to the market through the distribution channel. The collection brochures show the name of designer, knitter, and tailor under the brand name of Mehrbaf. Cofounders believe that it will be helpful if they later on decide to establish a workshop of their own or continue their education or career elsewhere (Tayebat, 2018).

Sustainability of business

Besides the lack of governmental support, the current economic difficulties and the increasing cost of raw materials have also caused problems for Mehrbaf. However, after seven years of experience, Tayebat stays optimistic about their production and market demand at the moment; the company is not making profit for further expansion of business but is able to pay the salaries of current employees and regular costs. Over the last two years, the founders have applied for loans from the banks and governmental funds that are supposed to support entrepreneurship, but still no positive response has been received (Tayebat, 2018).

Innovation

Mehrbaf has been always committed to avoiding out-of-date traditional business methods. They started with a comprehensive and detailed plan with a vision of three 5-year periods. For this, they've got consultancy services from young academic business and financial experts as well as educated art and fashion designers.

Legal constraints and challenges

According to Tayebat, the entrepreneurship administration of Cooperatives, Labour and Social Welfare Ministry merely focuses on theoretical projects.

Besides, there are two other foundations of Entrepreneur Women and Entrepreneurship Development; yet there is a serious lack of legal coverage for them to monitor the workshops and entrepreneurship centres in a definite structure. She also expects supporting regulations such as a different tax system, lower insurance fees for social entrepreneurs, or a special bonus for attending trade fairs or seminars (Tayebat, 2018).

Contribution of international organizations

International institutions can certainly help the development of such businesses. However, due to special concerns of the state, Mehrbaf has always refused the aid proposals of international institutes, though it could be very useful especially at the beginning of their work. Up to now, they have only relied on the support of their local companions. Fortunately, many economic experts have positively evaluated the work of Mehrbaf, their acceptance in the current Iranian market, and economic self-efficacy. However, they have not received any positive feedback and support from the government so far.

Despite the lack of governmental support, Tayebat is serious in continuing this business. She puts her hopes in the contribution of civil society and those who are fundamentally concerned about social harms such as unemployment, and female empowerment (Tayebat, 2018).

Dastadast

Dastadast is a non-governmental non-profit institution. It is one of the first Iranian online markets that is administered as a social business. Faezeh Derakhshani – one of the founders of Dastadast – describes their working model, activities, and perspectives.

Targeted social impact: empowerment of the handicrafts producers with special concentration on neglected groups

Dastadast is a social enterprise with the aim of empowering local producers of handicrafts to achieve a sustainable social status. According to Derakhshani (2018), their effort is to expand the market and provide the opportunity for the producers so that they do not depend solely on small local markets of their town or village any more. With Dastadast, they can supply their handicrafts all over the country. Their ten-year mission is to support and empower thousands of women who are the breadwinner for their families. The motivation and encouragement of the founders for starting the work was introducing a new model of social activity with more sustainability and moving away from charity models. Derakhshani believes that the charity model leaves some social and personal harms behind; thus it should be limited to very special cases (Derakhshani, 2018).

Nature and registered framework of business

The organization is registered as a non-profit NGO; thus they are completely committed to spending the profit of the work on improving and expanding the services. In her words, however, a social business or enterprise necessarily uses entrepreneurship methods for solving a social problem, while an NGO does not have such a commitment. Regulations are supposed to be supportive and different from those of for-profit companies. But for taxes, for example, these regulations are not practically executed. The governing rules around the NGOs are not fully consistent with the nature of social businesses. That's why they have not reached a sustainable point and, as Derakhshani states, their business still needs to attract more financial resources (Derakhshani, 2018).

Commitment to the targeted social impact

Dastadast provides different degrees of transparency for different stakeholders. Members, volunteers, and sponsors receive financial reports. The reports are not released to the public as the founders believe that, in the current business environment of Iran, revealing their income statistics will put them in loss. Volunteer working is a fundamental concept of this organization and all members, even the general directors, spare many hours of volunteer working. Derakhshani says that their project is based on the goals of sustainable development, observing the ten principles of fair trade, and that they have never neglected social principles to gain financial profit. Their fair trade procedure is not certified by any organization, because Iran is not a member of FLO international. However, their commitment to the fair trade principles helps them not to lose their framework of values despite numerous economic problems (Derakhshani, 2018).

Innovation

Dastadast applies new technologies such as customised apps designed for the communication and the progress of their work. In their mind, however, innovation is not limited to technology. Complete recognition of cases they are dealing with and the current learning feature through the all organizational procedures enables the team to find innovative solutions for the problems that they face.

Legal constraints and challenges

Derakhshani says that they have to deal with more regulations and constraints compared with the for-profit companies. Not only did they have to get all the required permissions for registering the NGO in the first place, but also they still need to go for many different kinds of licences for running the business, and settle up the tax issues that totally depend on the personal views of auditors (Derakhshani, 2018).

Founders of Dastadast expect the government to facilitate the registration of social businesses and offer them tax exemptions. At present, they need to go through a huge bureaucratic procedure to get the required permissions that in an ideal situation could be avoided. These procedures cost much time and money, thus may stop one pursuing non-profit activities.

Derakhshani believes that the role of the civil society activists is also significant. Some of the civic activists use the banner of social business as a covering for their charity or for-profit financial activities, while the idea and insight underlying this concept is quite different. She also mentions the following as solutions for improving the current situation:

- introducing the true meaning of social business in journal articles, speeches, and special events.
- forming councils for consultation, mentoring, and related training courses.
- granting social businesses with the social responsibility budgets of private companies (Derakhshani, 2018).

Perspective

Derakhshani has no clear perspective on the future because of the unfavourable economic conditions, and lack of governmental support. According to her, their work is being ignored in Iran. Since the cofounders were all young women, people tend to consider them weak and emotional. On the other hand, it is difficult to find sponsors for non-profitable social activities which simultaneously pursue economic projects. In the meanwhile, she thinks that funds from international institutions that are acknowledged by the Iranian government could be effective support for social businesses.

Keshmoon

Keshmoon is an online marketplace for saffron with social and environmental concerns. The start-up links saffron farmers of Qaen village to potential buyers. The primary version of the website was launched in Spring 2017. After attracting the initial investments, Keshmoon started its serious activity in February 2018. Mohammad Ghaempanah – one of the founders of Keshmoon – comes from a farming family and resides in the region. The main motivation behind the business is to help farmers survive the water scarcity problem. Qaen is a village in South Khorasan province, in which farmers used to take their water from Qanats that were traditional sustainable structures for extracting underground water. These days however, deep wells are used instead of Qanats as they turned dry. The level of underground waters in Qaen is lowered by half a metre per year which leads to water scarcity and more salinity. Saffron corms are sensitive to the salt in water. So, the farms were abandoned and the farmers left their job one by one (Ghaempanah, 2018).

Targeted social impact: providing a platform for direct selling of saffron and improving environmental sustainability

The founders of Keshmoon took some facts into consideration. First: saffron farming was the traditional job of all families in the region. But due to the above described conditions, the young generation does not think about farming any more. Secondly, saffron is one of the world's most expensive and valuable spices. Thirdly the plant does not need so much water to grow. Fourthly the supply chain of saffron traditionally consists of several mediators; thus little wage or profit remains for the farmers. In addition, the quality of the product which is transferred to the consumer in a traditional trading system is not uniform and standardised.

In the Keshmoon online market, the farmers are classified based on their cultivating methods (conventional or organic), the quality of product, skill, knowledge, and the background of the farmer. By registering in Keshmoon, farmers are obliged to modernise their irrigation model under the supervision and support of Keshmoon experts. This will reduce water consumption and improve the sustainability of the water resources. All details are available for the buyers in the farmers' profile pages while the Keshmoon team keeps full supervision of the quality of the product and the production process. According to Ghaempanah, depending on the quality of each farmer's products, this system increases their revenue by 5–70% (Ghaempanah, 2018).

Nature and registered framework of business

The start-up has been registered under the title of 'Nik Kava Afra' as a privately held company and is located in the Science and Technology Park of Qaen in South Khorasan. Encouraged by the Science Park, it is moving towards converting its legal status to a knowledge-based enterprise that will bring advantages such as tax exemption for the company.

According to Ghaempanah, the first step for Keshmoon was choosing a good mentor that has a key role in the progress of start-ups. Considering the fact that saffron is a product with an international market, different markets such as China, India, Iran, Arabic countries, Europe, and Northern America were studied. Based on the selling price of saffron, observation of social-environmental issues by the final consumers, popularity of online shopping, and so on, the European market was targeted at the beginning. After the customer discovery phase, the founders applied for funds from some European accelerators, but they faced visa problems. The team was accepted to enter the first course of Iran's Know-Tech competitions sponsored by Sharif University of Technology. Although they did not succeed in working with the Know-Tech team, Ghaempanah refers to this as an important step in their self-confidence increasing and the development of the Keshmoon network. Later on, they applied for other accelerators in Europe such as Techstars. These attempts also did not lead to attracting an investor, but a great deal of learning and progress for the team. Finally, the team decided not to spend more cost and time on the European market and turned its focus on the Iranian market (Ghaempanah, 2018).

Legal constraints and challenges

For any start-up, the most important factor is the proper team formation. For a start-up team, mutual understanding, accurate task division, teamwork spirit, and synergies are the main challenges as the team has to grow in a short time with very low tolerance for making mistakes.

Besides the internal challenges, the external structure, including the exhausting bureaucracy of the governmental agencies for getting permissions, is a serious problem. These are not clearly determined step-by-step procedures. On the other hand, the procedures of different governmental agencies are not coordinated. Sometimes, they put the entrepreneurs in different and conflicting paths that waste a great deal of time and cost.

Another important problem is internet censorship. Keshmoon spent lots of time and money to build their buyer network on Telegram, and suddenly the government decided to block this social network. As stated by Ghaempanah (2018), they are not able to spend more time and money to shift their audience to another social network and all of the sudden their whole investment was wasted.

Ghaempanah refers to Iran's international political challenges as another important problem which has affected all of their commercial relationships. Saffron is a product with international customers and the Keshmoon market planned for global customers at the beginning. Currently though, the road to the international market is blocked.

Despite their efforts, no positive feedback has been received from international institutions such as UNDP Iran. Ghaempanah believes that structure of these organizations in Iran is not efficient and very similar to the governmental organizations meaning relationships work to access aids and support for a specific project, not a pre-set regulation or eligibility criteria system (Ghaempanah, 2018).

Conclusion

This study evaluates the root causes of poverty spread in Iran and the potential of civic activists' engagement in the process of sustainable development. A survey on Iranian experts' point of views leads to the conclusion that inequality rising from the dominant neoliberal system, general structural and management problems, financialisation of economy, lack of investment in industrial productive sectors, and, as a result, unemployment are the main causes of poverty in Iran. While many institutional economists focus on the political-economy approach, some others underline the role of society and organizing a powerful civil society to confront poverty. Civic institutions are expected to come up with solutions that are both feasible and society reliant. From here, the idea of promoting social businesses is suggested as a solution of civil society engagement. In order to have a realistic picture of social businesses in Iran, their missions, challenges, successes, and failures were discussed through interviews with the cofounders of three different organizations. These organizations are established and managed by a few individuals beyond the target groups that are expected to experience change. This means that, similar to the BOP approach and unlike other forms of social economy (such as cooperatives), an external agent is active here. However, it is interesting to note that despite involvement of external agents, all three interviewed organizations are working within local boundaries and focus on making social impact in the societies that they live in. Here is a clear distinction between the social business approach and BOP 1.0 and BOP 2.0 that mainly focus on the involvement of large corporations. Community-centric approaches that focus on building self-reliant societies could be however classified as BOP 3.0 strategies. One exception is the NGO Dastadast, but any BOP strategy should have a profit-seeking nature and, more importantly, be independent of continuous financial aid. Mehrbaf and Keshmoon are both private owned enterprises that in the long term cannot rely on capital injection from external sources. These two organizations seem to struggle more severely with their sustainability challenge. That's why they are taking the factor of innovation very serious, and, in the case of Keshmoon, look for a new business model of knowledge enterprise to take advantage of governmental support.

As stated by experts and the interviewed founders of social businesses, development and promotion of this model in Iran requires the establishment of an institutional framework and a cultural context. As highlighted by the three interviewed parties, in the absence of a special legal structure for social businesses, they lack governmental support which leads to sustainability challenges. Therefore, governmental support like tax exemption, while keeping an independent surveillance system to monitor their commitment towards primary social goals, is necessary.

This study lines up with the definition of social business as transformation and suggests that in the current situation of neoliberal domination of Iran's economic system, social businesses could work as a model of positive civil resistance that targets market and job creation. Unlike the usual resistance approaches, it is a positive impact making approach A social business targeted at poverty reduction means job creation and passing the real agency (at least in the long term) to community members.

In the development of social businesses to reduce poverty, the media have a great role to play. Furthermore, the consumer role of civil society members is very important. Citizens (consumers) can enter the market as the most influential actors in the social inclusion project.

Given the extent of structural inequalities and domination of a sort of individualism in the economic sphere of Iran, promotion of social businesses that seek profit and at the same time put a social impact such as poverty reduction in the core of their activities would be difficult and their sustainability is subject to uncertainty. This also has roots in the problematic overall business environment of Iran in which running a healthy productive business, even if it is for profit only, may face serious challenges. Therefore, the onus is still on the government to improve the general business environment to the benefit of productive activities and give the civic organizations more latitude to manoeuvre. Yet, there are civic activists who have not delayed their efforts in the hope of fundamental structural changes and, relying on their own moral commitments, they pursue poverty reduction in the micro levels of their surroundings. In fact, the purpose of such social activism is to eliminate clearly remediable injustices, as Amartyia Sen writes in the preface of *The Idea of Justice*: 'What moves us, reasonably enough, is not the realization that the world falls short of being completely just – which few of us expect – but that there are clearly remediable injustices around us which we want to eliminate' (Sen, 2009, p. vii). A common motivation that was observed behind the activities and words of the founders of the three organizations is their commitment to love their home-place. There is a precious knowledge of each community's culture, way of living, economic priorities, and social values that roots in their long-term history. Being equipped with such knowledge is potentially a key to the sustainability of these businesses.

Notes

1 20/3/2016 to 20/3/2017 using the Gregorian calendar.
2 20/3/2018 to 20/9/2018 using the Gregorian calendar.
3 20/3/2015 to 20/9/2016 using the Gregorian calendar.
4 Assistant Professor at Economic Department, Alzahra University.
5 20/3/2017 to 20/3/2018 using the Gregorian calendar.
6 Faculty member of Tehran University.
7 Head of economy group at Allame Tabatabai Universityand and former Deputy Minister of Cooperatives, Labour and Social Welfare.
8 Muhammad Yunus is a Nobel Peace Prize winner, economist, and social entrepreneur.

References

Agnihotri, A. (2012). Revisiting the debate over the bottom of the pyramid Market. *Journal of Macromarketing, 32*(4), 417–423.

Bonsu, S. K., & Polsa, P. (2011). Governmentality at the base-of-the-pyramid. *Journal of Macromarketing, 31*(3), 236–244.

Borzaga, C., Galera, G., & Nogales, R. (2008). Social enterprise: a new model for poverty reduction and employment generation. *Bratislava, Slovakia: United Nations Development Programme Regional Bureau for Europe and the Commonwealth of Independent States.*

Chmielewski, D. A., Dembek, K., & Beckett, J. R. (2018). 'Business unusual': building BoP 3.0. *Journal of Business Ethics*, 1–19.

Cieslik, K. (2018). The quandaries of social entrepreneurship studies – a discursive review of the discipline. *Review of Social Economy, 76*(3), 352–376.

Crabtree, A. (2007). Evaluating 'The Bottom of the Pyramid' from a fundamental capabilities perspective. *Copenhagen Business School Centre for Business and Development Studies Working Paper, 1*, 1–22.

Dasgupta, P., & Hart, S. L. (2017). Creating an innovation ecosystem for inclusive and sustainable business. *Base of the Pyramid 3.0: Sustainable Development through Innovation and Entrepreneurship*, 96.

Defourny, J., & Develtere, P. (2009). The social economy: the worldwide making of a third sector. *The Worldwide Making of the Social Economy. Innovations and Changes*, 15–40.

Dembek, K., Sivasubramaniam, N., & Chmielewski, D. A. (2019). A systematic review of the bottom/base of the pyramid literature: cumulative evidence and future directions. *Journal of Business Ethics*, 1–18.

Derakhshani, F. (November 10, 2018). Personal interview.

Garrette, B., & Karnani, A. (2010). Challenges in marketing socially useful goods to the poor. *California Management Review, 52*(4), 29–47.

Garshasbi, A. and Yusefi, M. (2016). Assessment of international sanctions on Iranian macroeconomic variables. *Journal of Research in Economic Modeling*, 7(25), 129–182.

Ghaempanah, M. (December 22, 2018). Personal interview.

Industrial Management Institute. (2017). Gozareshe vizhe hamayeshe sherkathaye bartare Iran [Special report of top Iranian companies conference]

Iran's Statistics Centre. (2017). Chekideye natayeje tarhe amargirie nirooye kar bahar 96. Retrieved from https://www.amar.org.ir/Portals/0/News/1396/2_ch_ntank_96-1.pdf

Islamic Parliament Research Centre of the Islamic Republic of Iran. I.R.I. Const. (1989). Retrieved from https://rc.majlis.ir/fa/content/iran_constitution

Jazani, N., & Khatavakhotan, A. S. (2011). A new paradigm to evaluate the BOP population by considering the effects of inflation rate: a real case study. *International Journal of Social Science and Humanity, 1*(3), 235.

Karnani, A. G. (2006). *Mirage at the Bottom of the Pyramid*. William Davidson Institute Working Paper No. 835. Retrieved from SSRN: https://ssrn.com/abstract=924616 or http://dx.doi.org/10.2139/ssrn.924616

Khavand, F. (2018, December). Khate faghr dar Iran 1397 [Poverty line in Iran: 2018]. RADIOFARDA. Retrieved from https://www.radiofarda.com/a/commentary-on-poverty-line-in-iran/29651945.html

Khoshbin, S. (2013, April). Bozorgtarin gonah, faribe tohi dastan ast [The greatest sin is the deception of the poor]. TEJARATEFARDA. Retrieved from http://www.tejaratefarda.com/fa/tiny/news-18868

London, T. (2007). A base-of-the-pyramid perspective on poverty alleviation. *Ann Arbor: The William Davidson Institute-University of Michigan, Working Paper*, 1–46.

Madani, S. (2018, October). Mobareze ba faghr yek mas'aleye akhlaghi ast [Fighting poverty is a moral issue]. IRNA. Retrieved from http://www.irna.ir/fa/News/83081983

Meidari, A. (2018, October). 18 ta 35% mardom zire khate faghr hastand [18–35% of the people are below the poverty line]. ISNA. Retrieved from https://www.isna.ir/news/97080703284/

Office of Population, Labour Force and Census. (2019). Chekide va natayeje tarhe amargiriye nirooye kar bahar 1396 [Summery and results of labour cencus plan; Spring 2017] Retrieved from https://www.amar.org.ir/

Office of the High Commissioner for Human Rights (2012). Guiding principles on extreme poverty and human rights. *Human Rights Council Resolution, 21,* 11–18. Retrieved from https://www.ohchr.org/Documents/Publications/OHCHR_ExtremePovertyandHumanRights_EN.pdf

Omidi, R. (December 1, 2018). Personal interview.

Peredo, A. M., Montgomery, N., & McLean, M. (2018). The BoP business paradigm: what it promotes and what it conceals. *Oxford Development Studies, 46*(3), 411–429.

Prahalad, C. K. (2002). The fortune at the bottom of the pyramid. *Strategy+ business,* 26.

Prahalad, C. K. (2009). *The Fortune at the Bottom of the Pyramid: Eradicating Poverty Through Profits, Revised and Updated 5th Anniversary Edition.* Upper Saddle River, NJ: FT Press.

Prahalad, C. K., & Hammond, A. (2002). Serving the world's poor, profitably. *Harvard Business Review, 80*(9), 48–59.

Raghfar, H. (November 24, 2018). Personal interview.

Raghfar, H., Babapour, M., Yazdanpanah, M., (2016.) Survey on the relationship between economic growth, poverty, and inequality in Iran during five-year development plan. *Quarterly Journal of Applied Economic Studies in Iran (AESI), 4*(16), 59–79. Retrieved from http://imi100.imi.ir/ConferencesDocs/file%20kholase%20gozaresh%2097-4%20final.pdf

Sen, A. K. (2009). *The Idea of Justice.* Harvard University Press.

Shahbazian, A., Abdollahi, M., Einian, M., Kaviani, Z. (2018a). Estimating the poverty line for the first six months of 1397, *Parliament Research Centre of IRI.* Retrieved from http://rc.majlis.ir/fa/report/download/1090439

Shahbazian, A., Abdollahi, M., Einian, M., Kaviani, Z. (2018b). Iran's Poverty Line in 1395, A Review on Calculation Methods, *Parliament Research Centre of IRI.* Retrieved from https://rc.majlis.ir/fa/report/download/1089090

Shargh Daily. (2018). Agahiye ajibe yek markaze daneshgahi baraye bahrekeshi az koodakane kar [The strange advertisement of a public university about child exploitation].

Shariati, S. (2018, October). Danesh alayhe faghr [Knowledge against poverty]. Iran newspaper. Retrieved from http://www.iran-newspaper.com/newspaper/page/6915/10/488152/0

Simanis, E., & Hart, S. (2008). The base of the pyramid protocol: toward next generation BoP strategy. *Cornell University, 2,* 1–57.

Taee, H. (December 5, 2018). Personal interview.

Tayebat, N. (November 24, 2018). Personal interview.

Tsd.cbi.ir. (2019). Retrieved from https://tsd.cbi.ir/DisplayEn/Content.aspx

Yunus, M., Moingeon, B., & Lehmann-Ortega, L. (2010). Building social business models: lessons from the Grameen experience. *Long Range Planning, 43*(2–3), 308–325.

Index

Printed in the United States
by Baker & Taylor Publisher Services